LEISURE MANAGEMENT

BILL TANCRED AND GEOFF TANCRED

Hodder & Stoughton
LONDON SYDNEY AUCKLAND

British Library Cataloguing in Publication Data
Tancred, Bill
　Leisure management.
　I. Title　II. Tancred, Geoff
　790.06

　ISBN 0-340-55649-8

First published 1992

© 1991 Bill Tancred and Geoff Tancred

All rights reserved. No part of this publication may be reproduced or transmitted in any form or by any means, electronic or mechanical, including photocopy, recording, or any information storage and retrieval system, without permission in writing from the publisher or under licence from the Copyright Licensing Agency Limited. Further details of such licences (for reprographic reproduction) may be obtained from the Copyright Licensing Agency Limited, of 90 Tottenham Court Road, London W1P 9HE.

Typeset by Wearside Tradespools, Boldon, Tyne and Wear
Printed in Great Britain for the educational publishing division of Hodder & Stoughton Ltd, Mill Road, Dunton Green, Sevenoaks, Kent by St Edmundsbury Press Ltd

Theory has no practical presuppositions, but practice always presupposes some theory. Ultimate values, for example, must first be simply seen and understood before we can do anything about them. Practical reason alone, in the absence of pure insight, is left without any stable grounds and must fall prey to random desires and interests

　　　　　　　　　　　　　　　　　　　　　　　　　　　　　　　John Wild.

◆ Contents ◆

Acknowledgements	iv
Preface	v
Leisure: Its nature and significance	1
Decision-making and communication: their role in leisure management	11
Leadership, group dynamics and team building: implications for the leisure professional	25
Leisure marketing: the marketing mix	41
Leisure marketing: research, segmentation and targeting	69
Leisure management	85
Trends in the health and fitness business	103
Joint provision and dual use of facilities for sport and recreation	119
Useful addresses	133
References	134
Index	137

◆ Acknowledgements ◆

We would like to thank all those professional colleagues who shared their experiences and provided information for this book and to express our appreciation to the publisher's reviewers; their contributions can be found at many points in the book.

Thanks are also due to the University of Sheffield and to Manchester College of Arts and Technology for their constant support. We are especially grateful to our wives, Angela and Jane, who showed understanding and patience whilst we pursued this book and to Lyn Murphy and Jane Tancred for their secretarial assistance. Any book is built on the contributions of many people, acknowledged and unacknowledged. We are grateful for the opportunity to join with them in the development of the important field of leisure studies.

◆ Preface ◆

This book is an introduction to the study of leisure. It is intended to raise some important issues and to provide an in-depth overview of some exciting developments in the growing field of leisure services.

The leisure boom has resulted in an explosive growth in leisure time activities. It has certainly become a major industry in the UK and is a good indication of how Britons now pursue the 'good life' beyond work and home.

Considerable growth and development has taken place in the leisure service industries. A larger range of leisure services and recreation sources, increased leisure awareness, the availability of more free time and increases in expendable money have combined to produce a society more orientated to leisure.

Recently the demand and the diversity have given rise to competition between leisure facilities and to interesting partnerships which blur the distinction between the public and the private sectors. The leisure facilities, for which local authorities used to be solely responsible, have become the subject of compulsory competition between private sector companies and the direct service organisations of local councils.

◆ Standards ◆

Whatever the leisure facility, and whoever is responsible for its management, a service is being provided which must satisfy an increasingly discerning user. Whether the user is a paying customer at a leisure centre or a visitor to a museum, he or she will expect certain standards to be met. The future success of the facility, and the organization responsible for its management, depends on the expectation being fulfilled. It is important that Leisure Managers remember this.

◆ Time ◆

Time will become an increasingly important resource, and its use will become an important factor in competition between businesses. We will see further extensions to opening hours for leisure venues and the development of 'time-freeing' ancillary services such as crêche facilities, and tighter 'time pledges' in connection with holidays and travel, for example, more guarantees of no delays at airports on pain of hefty compensation.

◆ TRENDS ◆

More radically, we see signs of a whole new attitude to leisure taking hold. In the 1990s, the attitude of the 1980s, which equated being busy with being worthy, and afforded high status to busy executives with mobile phones, may be on the wane.

The time may come when having leisure is perceived as an implicit statement about status – a return to historical attitudes towards leisure as the prerogative of the monied classes. This shift may be reinforced by growing concern about stress-related illnesses, directly attributed to constant time pressure and, if this happens, the 1980s could be seen as a temporary aberration rather than as the pattern for the future.

As leisure attains increasing priority in people's lives, consumers will choose narrower personal 'leisure portfolios' and their expectations and demands for a good service will increase along with their expertise.

This book will give an account of some basic concepts in leisure management, and of the professional competencies required by today's leisure practitioners. The book has been designed as a text for both higher and further education courses, and as a basic guide for leisure and recreation professionals in all types of leisure and recreation services.

We hope that you find it informative, interesting, and a contribution to your understanding of some of the major issues in leisure management.

Bill Tancred and Geoff Tancred

LEISURE:
ITS NATURE AND SIGNIFICANCE

The past half century has brought technological change at such an accelerated rate that our lives have been revolutionized. New industrial machinery, increased mobility, television and miracle drugs are just a few of the new and exciting influences that have changed the lives of many people throughout the world. As a result of such changes, there has been a marked increase in leisure time. People are working shorter hours and experiencing more leisure. Longer life expectancy through improved diet, exercise and drugs has resulted in longer retirement. Forecasters predict that by the turn of this century, most working people will spend only three to four week days at work with a corresponding increase in recreation and leisure time. Time for leisure can be seen as an evil as well as a blessing; it can hang heavy on people's hands; they can become bored or restless if they do not understand how to utilise free time.

There is probably a greater need at the moment for a definite balance between work and meaningful leisure and recreation than ever before. Therefore, leisure must be approached seriously: the pace of modern society demands it. It is part of the Leisure Manager's job to help people achieve this balance. We may be standing at the threshold of a leisure-oriented society with almost unlimited possibilities for the enrichment of human life through the constructive use of leisure time and professionals working in leisure must provide opportunities for individuals to express themselves in a productive manner that will not only benefit them but also society.

◆ LEISURE AND WORK ◆

Work and leisure produce different satisfactions for different people. As a result, we are likely to vary in our perceptions of the relationship between them.

Parker (1971) [1] developed a model that begins with relative freedom and constraint as the critical dimensions for understanding the work–leisure relationship. At the high constraint end of the continuum are work and meeting physiological needs, while at the high freedom end is leisure. In between are various work and non-work obligations that need to be met at some time and in some way, but that are not set out firmly.

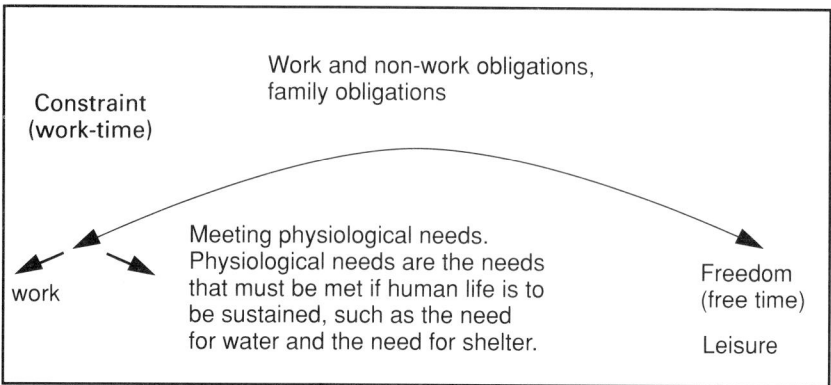

Fig. 1 The work — leisure continuum.

Parker proposed three types of relationship between leisure and work. The first, *identity*, describes a relationship in which the meanings, forms, associations, and satisfactions of work and leisure are the same. At the other extreme is a *contrast* between work and leisure in which leisure is different in order to make up for the deficiencies of work. The third possibility is that the two are essentially unrelated. It is a *separateness* that describes minimal contact or influence in which each is an arena of life with its own integrity.

◆ THE TERM 'LEISURE' ◆

There are many interpretations of the term 'leisure', and to many, leisure is taken as synonymous with recreation, which can be defined as a pastime, or activity from which the individual derives a pleasurable interest and enjoyment.

Perhaps the most common understanding of leisure is that it is the free time people have after they have taken care of their needs and after their work has been completed. Leisure time has been defined as

> '... that period of time at the complete disposal of an individual, after he has completed his work and fulfilled his obligations. Leisure hours are a period of freedom, when man is able to enhance his value as a human being and as a productive member of his society.' (Leisure Today, 1972) [2]

Today, leisure has an additional, and increasing, importance because more and more people turn to their free time for the social motivation and fulfilment which is missing from their jobs. It is not surprising that we hear so much about the importance of the 'quality of life'. Frustration and stress can, it seems, only be cured or improved by a 'leisure explosion'.

◆ THE TERM 'WORK' ◆

For many people today, work means earning one's living or earning money. Such an understanding can imply that there is little emotional content or self-respect in work and that it is both a 'necessary evil' and a means to a material end.

This view is encouraged by the great strides taken in modern technology. Higher standards of efficiency in business and production techniques have resulted in more concentrated levels of active work, yet have simultaneously intensified nervous and mental effort. There is considerable evidence that the fatiguing or deadening effect of some forms of occupation tend to polarize work and separate it from the rest of life, although individuals' reactions vary according to temperament.

We know that work can be important for many reasons other than earning a living. There are some occupations which provide the opportunity to enhance status, provide self-respect and open avenues for social contact and integration which might otherwise not have been available to the employee. Indeed, because work has been considered so important for so long a person's identity may be seen to depend on it.

Keeping workers happy is a major concern for employers. A company with unhappy workers will not be efficient. The crucial aim is to find ways to motivate workers who have been turned off by routine and who demand more say in what happens in the job. An employer can try several ways of keeping workers happy, such as introducing a shorter working week, or flexitime, and providing sports and crêche facilities.

Shorter working hours and a shorter working week appeal to workers. In their quest for more leisure, workers are becoming receptive to the idea of squeezing the same amount of work into a reduced number of days.

Proponents of the plan for a shorter working week argue that it will reduce absenteeism, save energy, reduce pollution, and give employees more time with their families. Opponents contend that the plan will increase moonlighting by employees working on days off, thereby reducing job opportunities for the unemployed. They further argue that it will lead to employee fatigue, bringing decreased productivity and more on-the-job accidents.

Many British companies have initiated programmes of flexitime. With flexitime, companies set certain 'core hours' in which employees are required to be at work. Basically, employees can vary their starting and stopping times so long as they put in the required total number of hours. Early risers can begin at eight o'clock and leave at four o'clock in time for tennis, choir, shopping or to pick up a youngster at school. Others may, if they wish, arrive at ten o'clock and work late.

Flexitime gives people much more freedom to organize their lives, reduces pressure on transportation systems, and improves productivity. Such a programme has proved to be especially successful with working mothers who like to get home early. Some people work extra hours early in the week, then leave early on Friday, giving them a long weekend. In addition, many companies who have introduced flexible working hours have reported higher employee morale and a lower absenteeism rate.

There are also some large organizations (such as British Nuclear Fuels Ltd. and the Civil Service) who provide leisure and sporting facilities at or near the work place. Families, retired employees, members' guests and associate members are the main beneficiaries.

◆ POTENTIAL PROBLEMS OF LEISURE ◆

Leisure that cannot be used constructively can be just as bad as no leisure at all. Some writers have even viewed leisure as a social problem. As long ago as 1929, Cutten [3] highlighted restlessness, the desire for excitement, the inability to be alone, lack of self-discipline, boredom, fatigue and lack of play experience as potential problems of unstructured free time.

Staley (1976) mentions that,

> 'we have in our society at the present time, almost no concept of preparing people for a life of meaningful, significant leisure. We have been culturally conditioned to getting personal satisfaction from a "job well done". We do not even know whether people can accept leisure as a resource for a satisfying way of life.' [4].

Today we are making great efforts to prepare ourselves and the younger generation for a satisfying life incorporating long periods of leisure, but there is still room for improvement. There is an urgent need for people to learn how to use time to relax and break free from the stresses of work. An individual must have a trained intellect and possess a wide range of skills to be able to choose and make informed decisions; constructive choices cannot be made unless the individual has the knowledge and emotional make-up to want to use leisure constructively.

Unfortunately many people in senior positions or positions of some responsibility feel guilty when they have free time, they continue to work to avoid it and leisure becomes a problem. Leisure professionals must help them overcome their guilt and show them that obtaining more leisure and using it actively and creatively can be an effective means of overcoming stress and related difficulties.

◆ EDUCATION FOR LEISURE ◆

Far too many people today are unprepared for leisure. Leisure hours must be used in a constructive manner rather than destructive if individuals are to be healthy and strong and society is to be peaceful. Individuals need guidance and support in personal development.

Preparation to enjoy increased free time has proved difficult for some people, because they did not develop many leisure skills when they were young. If leisure time is to be spent in free-choice activities, individuals should know what free-choice activities are available to them. Education should aim to enable people to use their leisure more purposefully and in an intelligent manner.

The use of leisure in a democratic society, will always remain a matter of personal choice for the individual. However, with the increased amount of leisure time, society should accept some obligations and responsibilities for making sufficient provision for leisure and for providing recreation facilities.

The appointment of community leaders such as teachers, sports development specialists, recreation advisors and others whose role is helping people to acquire and develop the various qualities and competencies needed for the wise use of leisure time, is an extremely important challenge.

As in any form of education, the main purpose of education for leisure, is to bring about certain desirable changes in pupils, such as changes in attitude, knowledge, skill and behaviour. Young pupils who are taught to use their leisure time productively, will enhance not only themselves but ultimately the community at large. The skill to use leisure productively is a skill for life.

So the best solution to the potential problems of leisure is education aimed at the young. This is improving all the time and leisure education is now part of the school curriculum. While the merits of the traditional physical education curriculum cannot be denied, many educators believe, quite rightly, that we must educate and involve pupils, not only on an activity level, but also on a personal and social awareness level. If pupils develop an awareness of the importance of leisure in society and a recognition of the significant values that it may contribute to their lives, then society in general will benefit.

The goal of the leisure educator is to instil in pupils the ability to formulate a positive leisure attitude and discover new leisure interests and activities for themselves. The educator's tool is a course that will help pupils identify an ideal leisure lifestyle and set realistic goals to meet this end.

◆ THE GOAL OF ◆
LEISURE TEACHING IN EDUCATION

The goal of leisure teaching is to expose children to a reservoir of different activities that are adaptable and pertinent to many different situations and environments. The pupil should be encouraged to include some activity daily, to have at his or her disposal activities that can be conducted either alone or with others, and activities that involve active participation as well as observation. These activities should be capable of sustaining a pupil through his or her lifetime.

Leisure education can help develop inherent feelings of identity and self-worth which can carry over to other educational processes and facilitate learning. Erikson (1950) stresses that involvement in play and leisure are an important part of the maturation process. He says that the play act is a function of the ego, an attempt to bring into synchronization bodily and social processes. Thus, developing satisfying play experiences helps all children to mature and make sense of their environment.

It is of paramount importance that teachers should stress that all individuals have enormous amounts of free time not devoted to meeting obligations. Teachers and parents must accept the responsibility of providing education so that children can develop inventories of skills that will be utilized in their avocational pursuits. If this is not done, the results can be very distressing. In the USA, for example, studies have noted that many children appear to lack the awareness, skills and internal drive to meet either their lifestyle needs or their vocational skill needs because they have learned to become too dependent on television. Other recreational alternatives must be taught to children so that they do not get attached to the television set as their major source of relaxation.

◆ GUIDE FOR LEISURE TEACHING ◆

It must be ensured that learning activities, materials utilized and the play environments provided are appropriate for the specific development age. The programmes selected should be widely based and provide the skills necessary for a child to engage in activities, either by himself or herself, or in small group settings.

Activities selected should be both active and passive. If children know only how to play in the presence of others, they are not prepared to deal with time on their own and although they may cope well when they are surrounded by others, when left on their own they lack ideas about how to fill their time.

Children need help in recognizing their competencies so they will develop the confidence to take a chance. Merely exposing children to activities and encouraging their involvement will not be enough. Children must feel a sense of competency if they are to risk failure. Parents and teachers must help children develop an internal locus of control. This can be done by selecting activities in which children will succeed, so when programming, one should take advantage of children's abilities and develop activities which will highlight their strengths, rather than their limitations. This will give children the confidence to engage in activities in which they are less proficient. It is also important that children be taught and motivated to try self-generated activities so they can begin to believe that their own effort influences their ability to perform in any context.

Intrinsic motivation (a drive from within the child, to participate in an activity for whatever personal reason, for example, satisfaction, joy) should be encouraged whenever possible. Research findings have suggested that when children have intrinsic motivation, learning, particularly conceptual learning and creative thinking, are dramatically increased.

Children should also be encouraged not to be dispirited by failure. Nearly everyone has inadequacies, and nearly all fail at some time in life. Children should be taught to interpret failure as feedback, indicating that more information is needed, as well as to focus attention on effort, rather than solely on personal ability and achievement.

◆ Developing a leisure ethic ◆

In today's work oriented society there is a real need to develop an ethic of leisure. Leisure literacy must be acquired by people if they are to use leisure time constructively. Leisure must be approached seriously and people's attitudes towards leisure must undergo profound changes. New forms of leisure must be encouraged that will stretch the mind, develop an individual's potential, and enrich their life.

A leisure ethic should be a set of attitudes, a value system and a way of helping individuals make decisions about leisure as well as foreseeing the consequences of those decisions. A major priority in the educational process should be the establishment of a leisure ethic. As Staley (1975) said, 'To reap the richest harvest from leisure, one must be conditioned and made ready for it.' [6].

◆ THE FUTURE ◆

Many challenges will face leisure professionals in the 1990s. The most important challenges of all are those of educating people to accept and use leisure and to develop a leisure ethic. Changing people's attitudes and encouraging people to place a higher value on leisure should be never-ending concerns of all professionals working in the fields of recreation and leisure education.

Ranked high on the list of biggest challenges for recreation and leisure agencies is the recognition that the traditional sources of financial support can no longer be relied upon. Some of us are already using alternative means of financing and operating our programmes. In the 1980s a wave of new political ideas swept the country, with the effects being felt both at national and local levels. Cutbacks in services became evident in education and local authority provision, including leisure centres, museums, libraries, and theatres, forcing Leisure Managers to become ever more resourceful.

Revitalizing the inner cities of Britain is a challenge a growing number of urban communities have already accepted. Changing and making cities attractive places to live and work will help attract private investment and provide a strong incentive for citywide and neighbourhood economic regeneration. Leisure Managers can help in the regeneration of our inner cities by developing derelict buildings as recreation centres and helping to stimulate local people to participate in community activity.

A further challenge for the recreation and leisure services industry is to improve the programming. Today's programmes too often consist of activities designed to consume time, and to fill idle hours. In their place, creative, positive leisure activities and experiences are required, to challenge people to change, to learn and to grow. Enlightened, bold leaders are needed to plan and guide people's development, rather than to organize activities based entirely on popular demand.

Leaders in the field of recreation must begin to think of recreation experiences in terms of human development. The main concern of recreation is not programmes, facilities, or activities but *what happens to people*.

Another extremely important challenge to the leisure services profession is that of meeting the leisure needs of women and special groups such as disabled and handicapped people, ethnic minorities and the unemployed. We must also respond to the challenge to make people recognize their leisure needs before they reach retirement, as the proportion of elderly people in the population is growing.

The 1990s will undoubtedly provide many challenges to those in the leisure services field. Since it will be a major element of the consumer economy, leisure will be highly valued rather than dismissed as preparation for work.

◆ Conclusion ◆

If the recreation and leisure services field is to realize its vast potential, professional leaders must meet high new standards. The complexities of a rapidly changing society will demand a level of expertise far greater than that which has served the profession in the past.

Professional leadership, job skill competencies, and the quality of educational programmes and experiences provided will not only have to be better but also more effective, if the field is to succeed in its quest for true professionalism. Most important of all, qualified managers will be vital to the leisure industry and we hope this book will help develop the professionalism of managers and give them the information they need to meet some of the challenges outlined.

◆ Discussion Questions ◆

1. Describe your interpretation of leisure. What is leisure?

2. Which of Parker's models of the work–leisure relationship best describes people you know? Give examples.

3. Why do some people fail to use their leisure time in a positive, constructive manner? What suggestions do you have for these people?

4. What does 'education for leisure' really mean? What is the major purpose of leisure education?

5. What would be the best possible developments in leisure in the future? What factors make it likely or unlikely that such developments will be realized?

◆ Case study ◆

You are the Manager of a large sports centre which is based in a very active community which appears to value leisure and active recreation opportunities. The Chief Leisure Officer has appointed you to be a member of a Long Term Planning Committee. You are asked to prepare a paper for presentation to the Committee. The title will be 'The Future of Leisure and Recreation in the 1990s'.

1. How would you go about preparing the paper and what would you expect your paper to find?

2. In addition, how would you respond to the challenge to make people recognize their leisure needs before they reach retirement?

DECISION-MAKING AND COMMUNICATION: THEIR ROLES IN LEISURE MANAGEMENT

The activities in which employees are engaged are the essence of any organization. Decision-making determines what these activities are and how they will be accomplished. It involves virtually all members of the organization, both as individuals and as members of groups.

Without a decision-making mechanism, an organization would collapse into a collection of individuals, each pursuing a different goal. For example, suppose a soccer coach made no decision regarding team tactics but simply said to his squad 'Okay, let's go for it!' They would all do whatever they felt was right with no team work and the overall performance of the team would be poor. However, if the coach was professional he would consider his own team's strengths and weaknesses and the other team's tendencies. In consultation with the players, he could then work out the game plan meticulously, taking into account current weather conditions and other variables. He would communicate his decision on particular tactics of play to the team members, to their mutual benefit.

Decisions can be made by groups as well as individuals. Some coaches for example, decide tactics after consulting with the assistant coaches before and during matches.

◆ DECISION-MAKING ◆

The above examples illustrate three important characteristics of decision-making:

- ◆ a decision can be made by an individual or a group
- ◆ a brief decision-making process can be both logical and complex
- ◆ information is an indispensable element of the decision-making process.

A decision integrates the actions of individuals and makes their efforts pay off in terms of group or organizational effectiveness. Naturally, success will rely on the individuals' training, their willingness to perform duties and to undertake responsibilities, and their motivation to work efficiently and effectively. Remember, decision initiates action. Indecisiveness or unnecessary delay in initiating action can lead to a loss of enthusiasm, a lowering of morale, and eventually an apathetic response.

Decisions are judgements: choices between alternative courses of action, none of which is completely right or wrong. Successful Leisure Managers should aim to make decisions at the appropriate time and to base decisions upon the best possible information. Decision-making is an inescapable responsibility. Managers will be judged by their superior(s) and staff on the quality of their decisions. A plethora of bad or short-term decisions will undoubtedly lead to a serious backlog of time-wasting problems.

Managing a team's performance during a regular series of tasks or during special projects, involves decisions relating to routine, individuals and teams. It is extremely important that:

- impulsive decisions are avoided
- informal reactions to situations needing decisions are investigated in order to ascertain team response
- information gathered reflects a variety of viewpoints
- instinct need not be disregarded but must be tested against the information gathered
- temptation or coercion into making premature or unnecessary decisions is resisted.

◆ Decision-making: ◆
People and Circumstances

Successful components of decision-making include self-discipline, perception, creativity, dynamism and considerable skill in handling both groups and individuals. Other factors involved in the process of decision-making are:

- change
- conflict
- the possibility of being wrong and therefore of being asked to justify the action taken
- having to contend with many conflicting facts.

Most people would rather avoid making a decision of any importance. The failure to make a decision is very often worse than the alternative and colleagues and subordinates in an organization are often frustrated or virtually at a stand-still due to a manager's indecisiveness.

◆ STYLES OF DECISION-MAKING ◆

There are four identified types of decision-making, namely: autocratic, persuasive, consultative and co-determinate.

◆ *Autocratic*   An autocratic decision is one taken by an individual without any consultation, or advice from others. The individual then imposes his or her decision on colleagues. For general everyday matters this style of decision-making is acceptable. The person making the decision often has charisma or is acknowledged to be the expert with a good track record so the decision made by him or her will usually be accepted easily. Individuals may moan, but they may also grudgingly accept that decisions made at a higher level must sometimes simply be handed down without the chance of discussion.

◆ *Persuasive*   This is quite different from the autocratic style of decision-making in that the manager uses his powers of advocacy to explain and justify his decision to his staff, subsequent to the decision being made. There is no negotiation. This can be perceived as dishonest, in so far as staff are manipulated by clever sales talk into accepting a *fait accompli*. Indeed, it would be dishonest if such a decision was disguised as consultation and such pretence should not be used, but it is a worthy type of decision-making in the right circumstances, and all of us use it in our daily lives.

◆ *Consultative*   A consultative decision is one taken by the manager, but only after consultation with staff. The manager obtains the ideas, suggestions and commitment of those involved, but also ensures the consistency of decision-making and conformity to established guidelines. This style encourages motivation and effectiveness.

◆ *Co-determinate*   A co-determinate decision is taken by a group of people acting together. The risk of inconsistency is inherent with this approach, and while encouraging collective responsibility, individual responsibility may be undermined. This is the only method available when no one party has clear decision-making authority. Examples of co-determinate decision-making are negotiation and 'management by committee'.

Decision-making about routine general matters should be delegated to members of your team. Doing this not only encourages staff growth and development but it also frees you for strategic issues.

Certain decisions will undoubtedly require your close attention. The following are examples of such decisions, paying attention to these issues should enable you to be more effective and efficient as a manager:

- ◆ Overall direction. Which markets should we be in? Markets change rapidly in today's society.
- ◆ Staff resources, such as the recruitment of new personnel, and the promotion or discipline of existing staff.
- ◆ Reviewing the structure of your department. Are we properly organized to meet our objectives and cope with our workload?
- ◆ Specialized skills, such as the provision of information and facilities to help those taking technical decisions.
- ◆ Planning. Can the team continue to operate cost-effectively to achieve organizational targets and objectives? There might also be a need to enquire whether there are any new projects to be implemented or planned and if so, what budget requirements are needed.

◆ Effective decision-making procedures ◆

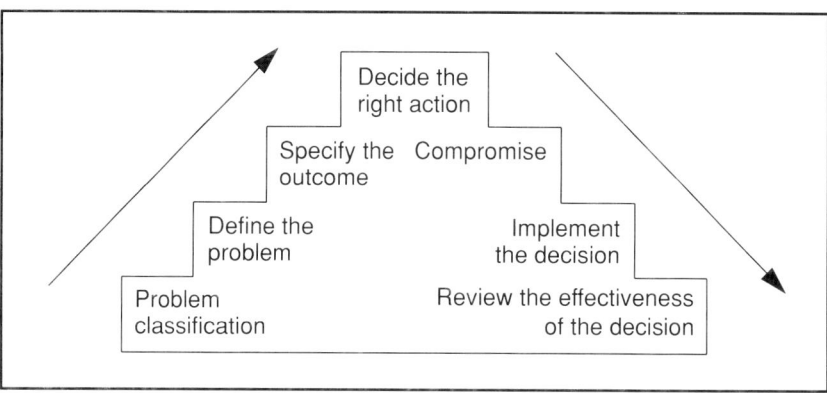

Fig. 2 Effective decision-making procedures

Decision-making has to be performed by managers. Decisions are not sudden, isolated events but rather ongoing and evolving processes that can be broken down into a series of steps. These steps are discussed briefly below and summarised in Figure 2. We have drawn on Drucker's work (1970) [7].

- ◆ *Problem classification*   Many problems are of a general nature which might occur everyday and can be solved by adapting the appropriate general rule, policy or principle. If, on the other hand, the problem is more complex, then it should be handled on its individual merits.
- ◆ *Define the problem*   The next step is to state the exact nature of the problem and check it against all the observable facts.
- ◆ *Specify the outcome*   Make clear precisely what the decision must achieve.

♦ *Decide*   At this stage, it is extremely important to decide the correct action to take, considering what is acceptable in the circumstances.
♦ *Compromise*   There always has to be a compromise, so endeavour to make the best decision possible by adapting it to the circumstances.
♦ *Implement the decision*   Formally appoint responsibility for carrying out the decision to those people capable of doing a first class job. Communicate with everyone who needs to know about the decision.
♦ *Review the effectiveness of the decision*   If evaluation of the decision is to be constructive, feedback must come back from all concerned and there must be a willingness to re-adjust or modify it, if it seems desirable.

In one large organization, a survey conducted at all levels, asked people what changes they would most like to see amongst managers. The most common reply was, 'that they should make decisions'. Many people surveyed also added remarks such as 'more clearly' or 'more rapidly', and there was a frequent comment that, 'it often does not matter which decision as long as they make one or the other'. Subordinates do require decision-making by their superiors. The highest of all risks to the organization is the risk of not deciding. This is apparent, for example, when a commercial organization slides into bankruptcy through failure to respond to market changes.

♦ GROUP PROBLEM-SOLVING TECHNIQUES ♦

One style of decision-making is to co-ordinate the efforts of the total group; rather than the manager making decisions, he or she leads the group in a self-governing atmosphere and the aim is consensus. If discussion is encouraged and a friendly climate prevails, all members should recognize that they have an opportunity *and a responsibility* to express their true feelings. If consensus cannot be achieved, compromises must be made until a mutually acceptable solution is found. Hence, even though some reservations may be retained, commitment to the final decision is felt by all group members and all are willing to try a particular mode of action and to help with subsequent evaluation. Such a procedure is usually conducive to high staff morale.

Managers may employ various group problem-solving techniques to stimulate participation in decision-making. Three methods of improving group decision-making are discussed below.

♦ *Brainstorming*   This is a technique first made popular in the 1950s and is most often used to generate alternative solutions for problems that are new to the organization or department and have major consequences. In brainstorming, the group convenes specifically for the purpose of generating alternatives. The members present ideas and are allowed to clarify them with brief explanations. Each idea is recorded and witnessed by all members, usually on a flip chart. To avoid the self-censoring of alternatives, no attempts to evaluate an idea are allowed. Group members are encouraged to offer any ideas that occur to them, even those that seem to be too risky or impossible to implement. In a subsequent session after the ideas have been recorded and distributed to members for review, they are evaluated. The intention of brainstorming is to produce innovative ideas and solutions by stimulating the creativity of group members and encouraging them to build on the contributions of others. Brainstorming does not provide the resolution to the problem, an evaluation scheme, or the decision itself.

◆ *Nominal group technique*   In nominal group technique, a group of individuals, who may or may not know each other, is brought together to address an issue. It is important to employ the services of a moderator to ensure that equal weighting is given to each idea, and to record the entire procedure. After the presentation of the issue to the group, each person compiles a written list of ideas, without discussion. Each person takes turns reporting one idea at a time to the whole group. These ideas are recorded on a flip chart as they are given. Members are also encouraged to add to the list by building on the ideas of others. Once all the ideas have been presented, the members may discuss them and continue to build on them or proceed to the next phase. This process can also be pursued without a face-to-face meeting by mail, by telephone, or by computer. Having a meeting however, helps members develop a group identity and puts interpersonal pressure on the members to perform their best in developing their lists. After discussion, members rank their preferences. This is performed by private vote in order to reduce any feelings of intimidation that may exist within the group. Group discussions about the results may occur after the voting has taken place, and this may continue to generate ideas. The generation—discussion—vote cycle can continue until the appropriate decision is reached. Two principal advantages exist in the nominal group technique. Firstly, it helps to overcome the negative effects of power and status differences among group members, and secondly, it can be implemented in problem exploration, alternative generation, and evaluation phases of decision-making. Its main disadvantage lies in the structural nature of the process, as the opportunity to put forward creative ideas may be limited.

◆ *Delphi technique*   This technique was introduced by the Rand Corporation (USA) as a method of systematically collecting the judgements of experts and it is used in developing forecasts. Primarily it is designed for groups who never meet face to face. The manager who requires the input of the group is the main figure in the process. When the participants have been recruited, the manager develops a questionnaire and sends it out for completion. When the completed questionnaires are returned, the manager summarizes the responses and reports back to the participants with another questionnaire. To generate the information required by the manager, this cycle may be repeated as many times as necessary. The Delphi technique is most helpful when experts are physically dispersed, where anonymity is desired, or when the participants are known to have problems of communication with one another. Another advantage of this method is that it avoids the problems of intimidation that may exist in decision-making groups. A disadvantage, however, is that the technique eliminates the beneficial results of direct interaction between group members.

In conclusion, the process of decision-making, as well as the content of the decision, is of paramount importance for success. An awareness of alternative decision-making procedures and processes can only be of benefit to the manager and his group.

◆ COMMUNICATION ◆

Communication occurs between individuals and groups and co-ordinates action. Its purpose is the sharing of information in an attempt to improve the effectiveness and smooth running of an organization at all levels. Communication is a vital component of the decision-making process, as has already been illustrated. If an organization lacks sufficient channels of communication then it is merely a collection of individual workers attending to separate tasks.

In a working environment the most important information to communicate relates to goals. Communication equips members with a sense of purpose and direction from a general level to an individual level of specific tasks. Task communication, originating from the personnel department, informs employees of their job duties, whereas information on organizational goals provides employees with a sense of how their activities are co-ordinated to fit into the overall picture. 'Feedback' information must also be given to employees. Often such information is passed on in performance appraisals.

◆ PRINCIPLES OF COMMUNICATION ◆

If communication within a local authority, leisure department or any other organization is to be consistently effective and efficient, it must be based on sound general principles. Managers and administrators must understand these principles and the reasons underlying them. The following five general communication principles should act as an aid for all leisure personnel.

◆ First principle: what, why, to whom, and when ◆

You must be quite clear what it is you are to communicate, why, to whom and when. It is important that you know the subject matter, or *what* is to be communicated, otherwise you will not be able to communicate adequately. For example, the secretary of a sports committee who has been present during a lengthy debate on a controversial matter will impart the feelings of the committee members in a report or letter more adequately than a person who has only the minutes of the meeting at his or her disposal.

In addition, you must know what you are trying to accomplish by communication, or *why* you are doing it, for if you do not know, how can you measure success? For example, you may be attempting to persuade or merely pass on information. Your success can be measured by the reaction or, the lack of reaction, of the recipient.

You must also know *to whom* you are communicating. As much information as possible about them must be known to you beforehand, so that your communication can be delivered in the most effective way. Find out for example, about their attitudes and knowledge of the subject matter, so that communication between you can be channelled smoothly and productively and in terms that are familiar to them.

Another important consideration is timing, or *when* to provide information. If you communicate too early it may produce forgetfulness and, on the other hand, if too late, the response will be hurried and mistakes may be made.

◆ Second principle: getting attention ◆

The second principle relates to the need to get the attention of the receiver. Some people will understand and act on oral communication whilst others must see written instructions, and still others may want to try things out before feeling certain of understanding. It is extremely important to ensure that from the very start attention is attracted. This applies to all forms of communication. Well designed stationery, and the prominence given to bright posters on notice- boards aimed at the public who visit the sports centre are examples of ways of getting attention. Sloppy presentation of information will lead people to ignore the message conveyed. Make sure that any later communications which amend previous ones attract the same attention. For example, if you, as a manager, amend a formal document by giving out a small, nondescript letter, this will in most cases cause you some problems.

◆ Third principle: ensure understanding ◆

You must endeavour to make sure that those who receive the communication understand it in the way you want them to. You need to think about individuals' backgrounds, training, education and previous experience. All of these points will affect the way they understand the message or information. In addition, people within a particular department or organization may use jargon which will confuse others. A case in point involved a local authority committee which had always met monthly and which decided to cut down the frequency of meetings. The Secretary of the Committee, informing all departments, used the term 'bi-monthly'. Some of the departments understood this to mean 'meeting in alternative months' whilst the remainder of departments read it as 'twice monthly'! If communication is to be successful and effective, then you must endeavour to communicate in the receiver's terms, or to help him or her to learn yours.

◆ FOURTH PRINCIPLE: MAKE THEM REMEMBER ◆

Special attention must be paid to the ability of the receiver to retain, recall and use information when required. Naturally, people's ability to memorize will vary and for those who do have difficulty, help should be forthcoming. Fortunately, much communication will be delivered to people who want to retain the information. A supervisor for a particular leisure service, for example, will want to make sure that he or she absorbs the information needed to make him- or herself more effective and efficient and to increase any chances of promotion. This person will also want to acquire information so that he or she is able to contribute to discussions in an informed way and to report back to subordinates as clearly as possible. In order to help subordinates, you must communicate in such a way that memory retention is enhanced and you must take account of the reasons people forget. One of these reasons is called 'fading', which is the tendency for unused information to become hard to recall over a period of time. Another reason people forget is called 'blocking'. This happens when recent material crowds in to expunge older information.

To overcome these problems certain methods can be employed. For example, to avoid 'fading', information should not be given until such time as it is to be used and its understanding should be tested by questioning, discussion and involvement. It is important to remember that nothing should be taken for granted. To avoid 'blocking', communication should be in stages so that the person has an opportunity to absorb the information gradually. Make sure you explain the task step by step and only when the staff member shows that he or she understands and has grasped the first step, should the following step be introduced.

It is also important to bear in mind that people generally will tend to understand, accept and retain, information that is simple, logical and familiar to them and about which they have been forewarned, rather than information thrust upon them at the last minute. People also tend to understand information if they can see it as part of a whole.

◆ Fifth principle: measure effectiveness ◆

You must be able to measure the effectiveness of your communication. Feedback is of paramount importance. This may be easy in a simple working situation, because any breakdown in communication will reveal itself straight away. Breakdown in communication may occur even when effort and concentration have been put into ensuring that everyone understands and a drastic reorganization of a department or service might cause some difficult problems. Communication problems might exist where departments or services are spread in different localities or venues; the distance contributing to the difficulty of receiving sufficient feedback. Good communication is critical in the performance of a team or an individual. An understanding of potential breakdowns and barriers is essential to the improvement of organizational or individual communication.

◆ Communication: ◆
SOME ADDITIONAL CONSIDERATIONS

There is perhaps no excuse which is used to explain failures as often as 'lack of communication'. Whether this is an honest explanation or not, it is a weakness which should be eradicated. The quality and degree of communication in an organization is one of the key criteria on which an evaluation should be based.

Operating procedures and policies must be made clear, staff and members of the public kept informed, grievances made known to those in authority, and the rationale for administrative decisions communicated to all staff. Overlapping of responsibility must be kept to a minimum, conflicts resolved, money apportioned, equipment purchased, and the use of facilities co-ordinated.

Announcements of special events must be made, instructions for unusual programmes disseminated, social activities planned and transportation arranged. Meetings must be organized, times and places announced, information gathered and decisions made. None of this can happen without effective communication. It is a never-ending list. A lack of information will result in disappointments. Individuals who are outside communication channels feel left out and let down. A single missing link in a channel of communication can cause considerable inconvenience and on certain occasions, an operation can be disrupted.

An efficient communications system will convey information in all directions

— vertically, horizontally, and diagonally. In organizational terms, superiors must keep subordinates informed, subordinates must keep their superiors informed and peers must keep each other informed. Figure 3 shows how channels of communication may operate.

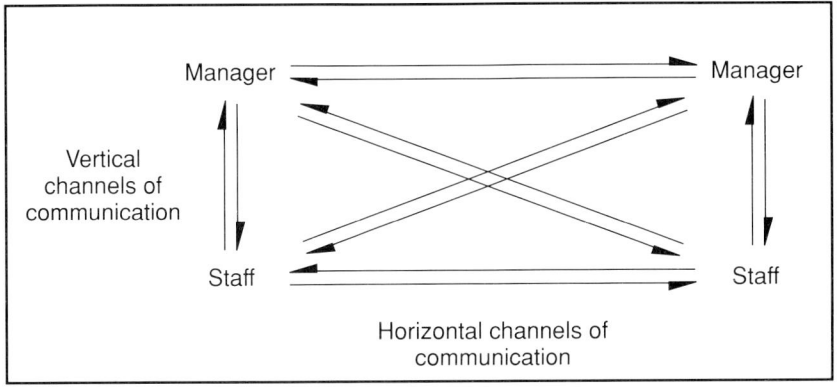

Fig. 3 The communication square

Mutual trust is characteristic of organizations in which individuals feel confident that they are being told the truth, that they will not be taken advantage of, and that they will be treated objectively and fairly. Nothing will solve communication problems, unless an atmosphere of trust prevails. The communicative function of informal social gatherings and social activities where people converge and have opportunities to talk must not be overlooked. Sometimes a manager may take staff away for a weekend in order to put important meetings on an informal basis. Very often, decisions are made and judgements influenced in such semi-social situations. Much business is completed over a beer or on the golf course, where the environment is most conducive to the free exchange of ideas. A quick and accurate flow of information and ideas throughout an organization is crucial. Co-ordinated effort toward common goals is not attainable without it. Part of this flow is written — management can specifically plan for the dissemination of written information and incorporate it into formal procedures and the design of forms and reports. Modern telecommunication systems and computing equipment greatly speed up this internal distribution of data.

However, it is important to bear in mind that subtle values and interpretations must still be conveyed orally. The oral approach is less direct than the written and managers must create situations in which full exchanges of thought can take place. A manager may help the flow of oral information by decentralization, establishing self-contained units, and placing staff close to operations. Where necessary, special staff such as liaison men or women and committees can be inserted in the structure. Contacts between people and departments can be fostered and reinforced by consultation across the organization.

Of course, some communication is spontaneous and so beyond management's immediate control. In this area, a manager simply tries to use the informal flow to supplement a network he has designed. Effective communication is of paramount importance, so much so, that we cannot call any organization fully designed unless it has given serious attention to communication networks.

◆ CONCLUSION ◆

One can see that both decision-making and communication are far more complex than they appear to be at first sight. However, for successful Leisure Managers, and section leaders in particular, the management functions of taking responsibility for decisions and controlling, as far as possible, the flow of information are of paramount importance. Therefore, an understanding of these two activities will undoubtedly help all those people aspiring to be successful in leisure management.

DISCUSSION QUESTIONS

1. Describe the decision-making style(s) of your friends and give some examples of their actions.

2. What information did you use in deciding to enter the education establishment that you are now attending?

3. Describe fully the purpose of organizational communication.

4. If communication within a large leisure department is to be consistently effective, and efficient, it must be based on sound general principles. Discuss these principles as they relate to leisure management.

5. Have you ever worked or studied in an organization in which communication was a problem? What were some of the causes of the problem?

◆ Case study ◆

The recreation staff at a small sports centre in a rural area consisted of two experienced staff and three young, relatively inexperienced instructors. They were completing a rather frustrating year in which they taught various physical activities from a syllabus furnished by the older of the two experienced staff. Since there was no appointed recreation head, the members worked independently of each other.

The older member of the two experienced staff had been there the longest (but was hoping for early retirement) and called periodic meetings of the group, but these meetings were generally merely reporting sessions. Little time was ever reserved for staff discussions.

The three younger instructors met informally once or twice and decided that they should seek some means of changing these conditions. They wished to become involved in the decisions that affected them and they felt that the syllabus could be improved. They discussed this with the younger of the experienced members of staff. He felt that he did not want to 'rock the boat'.

There was to be one more staff meeting before the end of the year. The three younger staff members met again to determine the best way to seek a change in the present procedure.

1. What are the issues in this case?

2. How should the three younger staff members seek involvement and change?

3. What principles of management are involved in this case?

Leadership, Group Dynamics and Team Building: Implications for the Leisure Professional

There have been numerous definitions of leadership offered, but none has won wide acceptance. We will define leadership in terms of both process and property. As a *process*, leadership is the use of noncoercive influence to direct and co-ordinate the activities of group members toward goal accomplishment. As a *property*, leadership is the set of characteristics attributed to those who are perceived to employ such influence successfully.

Management and leadership are not identical. Management relies on power stemming from formal position in a hierarchy to influence people, whereas leadership stems from processes of social influence. A leader can sometimes be formally appointed to head a group, but more often emerges informally from the ranks of the group according to a consensus of the members. A person may be a manager, but not a natural leader, a leader but not a manager, or both a manager and a leader.

Leadership is the skill of facilitating goal achievement. Whether the recreation professional guides an individual staff member in programme development or helps a team develop its vision, the quality of leadership will greatly affect whether or not these aims are achieved.

Professionals employed in the field of recreation and leisure are involved in a daily, dynamic exchange with the public; they must stimulate, educate, and motivate all sectors of the public to achieve full leisure satisfaction. It is extremely important, that the personnel of this 'people profession' possess the characteristics and skills to help participants bring out the best in themselves and their leisure. Leadership ability is thus basic to being an effective recreation professional.

◆ Effective Leadership: Qualities ◆

A good leader will be:

Dependable	Broadminded	Flexible
Fair	Creative	Enthusiastic
Sensitive	Ingenious	Intelligent

Self-confident   Tolerant   Candid
Persistent   Hard-working   Courageous
Sociable   Calm   Patient
Emotionally mature   Perceptive   Courteous

This is not a comprehensive list.

Reddin (1970) defines the effective leader as one who possesses

> 'sensitivity to the situation, which involves the manager's ability to accurately perceive a given situation, leadership flexibility which involves the leader's ability to change his style based on a given situation and situational management skill which is his ability to overcome resistance to change' [9].

◆ EFFECTIVE LEADERSHIP: ◆ FUNCTIONS AND RESPONSIBILITIES

The leader who is also an effective manager, in whatever type of business, will:

- Present positive image of goals and activities
- Set goals
- Communicate with staff
- Inspire/motivate
- Capitalize on individual skills and interests of staff
- Educate
- Adjust to staff member's individual capacities
- Co-ordinate
- Anticipate needs and problems
- Establish guidelines and structures
- Involve staff in decision making
- Establish climate for productivity
- Impart sense of security
- Acknowledge staff achievement
- Provide resources and information
- Make decisions on policies, procedures and approaches
- Summarize and restate individual and group goals
- Guide the evaluation process

This is not a comprehensive list.

◆ EFFECTIVE LEADERSHIP: TIME MANAGEMENT ◆

Poor time management has an adverse effect not only on the manager but on all those who come into contact with him or her. The Leisure Manager has four major resources — people, equipment, money and time. Time is irreplaceable. Time planning depends on a methodical and disciplined approach. Listed below are some points that can enable you to perform your duties more efficiently and effectively:

- ◆ List things that must be done according to priorities so that the most imperative are accomplished first. Keep track of time deadlines.
- ◆ Learn to say 'no' to requests that will take you beyond your scope of

duties. If you are unclear about the scope of your job description, you are likely to be distracted from your central purpose. Learning to delegate responsibility goes hand in hand with learning how to say 'no'.

◆ Know the method by which you best absorb and retain information. If you rely primarily on aural recall, then you may prefer to request oral reports from staff. If your visual retention is superior, then written reports would be preferable. A combination of both aural and visual information may even be better.

◆ To maximise the use of your time, know the times of day or night when you are generally at peak work performance. For instance, it would be unwise to schedule a critically important meeting of the Events Management Committee at the end of the day when your energy and concentration levels, and those of your staff, are low and flagging.

Effective time management often means the difference between a successful Leisure Manager and an unsuccessful one. Effective time managers use their time management habits every day. By concentrating on achieving goals, they feel less pressure and have a sense of control, thereby managing more effectively and efficiently.

◆ LEADERSHIP THEORIES ◆

The subject of leadership has received much attention in an effort to determine if there are any characteristics universal to effective leaders. Results have generally indicated that the intangibles of human interaction do not lend themselves to scientific study and that leadership is very much a dynamic, nonconcrete process that is specific to time, needs, and personalities. We now offer a brief overview of the observations made and theories proposed in the course of leadership research.

◆ LEWIN, LIPPITT AND WHITE ◆

Lewin, Lippitt and White (1939) identified three leadership styles and studied their effects on participants [10]. The three styles identified were autocratic, democratic and *laissez-faire*. The *autocratic* leader assumes an authoritarian stance, delegating no responsibility and permitting no input in decision-making. The *democratic* style invites staff and participant involvement in goal setting. Unlike the autocratic leader who tends to quash initiative, the democratic leader is inclined to bring out the best in others. In the *laissez-faire* style, the individual exercises no active leadership, but plays a permissive, passive role, serving solely as a resource if approached. Each of these styles can be appropriate depending on the leadership requirements of the situation. The same leader for instance, may exercise a *laissez-faire* attitude with a self-directed group at a drop-in centre, but exercise democratic leadership with a newly emerging youth social group.

◆ TRAIT THEORY ◆

Another approach, trait theory, attempts to classify those qualities inherent to leadership, viewing them as hereditary characteristics that comprise the 'born leader'. Trait theory seeks to determine the charismatic elements that cause people to be drawn to follow a particular individual.

◆ SITUATIONAL THEORY ◆

The situational theory of leadership stresses that leadership is dependent on:

- ◆ what the group seeks to accomplish
- ◆ the nature of the existing organizational structure
- ◆ how the individual's characteristics and skills complement the group goals and the organizational structure.

If, for example, a performance troupe's immediate concern is fundraising for their touring show and the organizational structure of their sponsoring agency encourages individual initiative, the individual with public relations or profit-making ideas will probably become a leader. However, that same individual will not necessarily remain a leader when the needs of the troupe turn to theatre production skills. The term 'emergent leadership' has been used to define this turnover in leaders, as each leader emerges in response to a particular situation for which his or her skills are suitable.

◆ CONTINGENCY MODEL ◆

Fiedler's (1967) contingency model of leadership effectiveness is similar to the situational theory in that it defines leadership as being 'contingent' on the situation itself [11]. The variables include:

- ◆ the leader–group-member relationship
- ◆ the type of goal to be achieved
- ◆ power position (leader's place in the organization).

Fiedler divides leadership into task-oriented and relationship-oriented styles. *Task-oriented* styles are primarily concerned with the quality of the work produced, whereas *relationship-oriented* styles emphasize the quality of the group interaction process leading up to the task achievement. In leading a hiking group for example, the recreation leader who stressed the acquisition of information and the completion of given assignments would be considered a task-oriented leader. On the other hand, a recreation leader who was primarily concerned with the establishment of group rapport among the hikers and the effects of the hiking experience on their social and emotional maturity would be viewed as a relationship-oriented leader. On this model, the success of recreation leaders is dependent on whether their task-oriented or relationship-oriented styles are appropriate to the type of leader–group–member relationship, task structure and power position existing in their specific situation. An effective leader should have a blend of both approaches.

The relationship between task-oriented and relationship oriented styles can be shown on a grid, see Figure 4. The horizontal axis of the grid represents a manager's concern for production (results) while the vertical axis represents a concern for people (relationships). Each axis is on a scale of 1–9. A manager may have varying degrees of concern for either production or people [12].

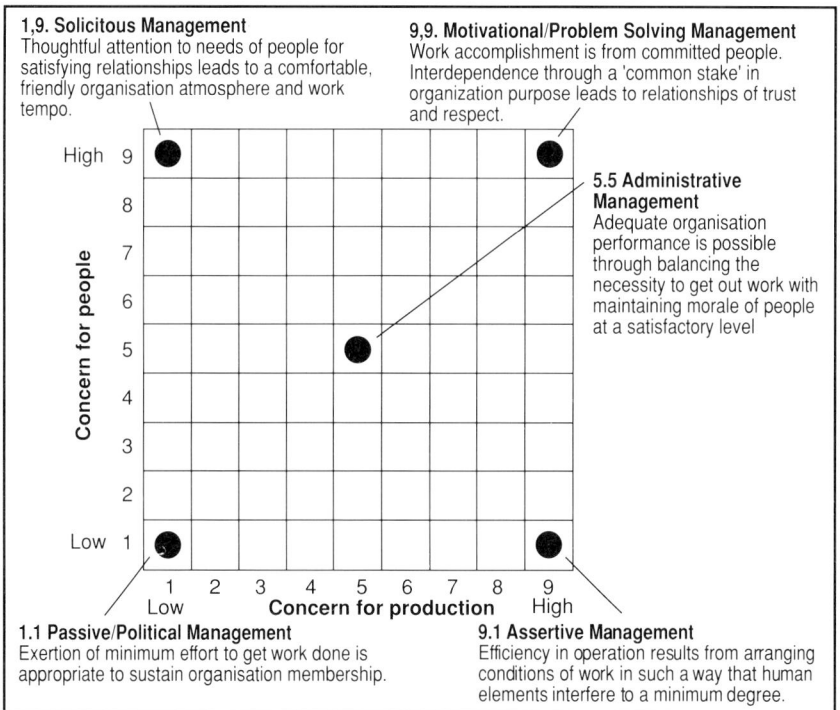

Fig. 4 The managerial grid (Based on Blake, R and Mouton J., The New Managerial Grid. Houston: Gulf Publishing, 1978).

Some of the attributes belonging to each of the five named positions are as follows:

◆ PASSIVE/POLITICAL MANAGEMENT: GRID POSITION 1/1 ◆

Passive behaviour:

- ◆ Will do no more than what is required.
- ◆ Any change will be resisted.
- ◆ If not checked, 'slackness' will result.

Political behaviour:

- Is very concerned about status.
- Is prompt to criticise.
- Quick to draw attention to the faults of others.

◆ Solicitous management: grid position 1/9 ◆

- Concerned about people.
- Wants to be popular.
- Evades open conflict.
- Praises achievement to the point of flattering.
- Not too concerned over slackness or poor performance.
- Has a certain tendency towards 'Management by Committee'.
- Always tries to be helpful.

◆ Administrative management: grid position 5/5 ◆

- Nearly everything done by the book.
- Keeps up the existing system.
- Conscientious rather than creative or innovative.
- Steady and has an adequate balance between concerns for production and people.

◆ Assertive management: grid position 9/1 ◆

- Requests that things are done in his or her way.
- 'Tells' instead of trying to 'listen'.
- Does not worry too much about other people's feelings or opinions.
- Any challenge will result in an aggressive response.
- Continual staff checks.

◆ Motivational/problem-solving ◆ management: grid position 9/9

- Agrees goals and expects achievement.
- Monitors performance against goals.
- Supports members of staff to find solutions to poor performance.

- Confronts conflict calmly.
- Agrees and monitors action plans.
- All delegation is made clearly.
- As and when needed, decisions will be taken and staff will be consulted.

You will see a variety of behaviour shown by your professional colleagues, your clients, the administrative and ancillary staff and other people with whom you come into contact virtually everyday. In each situation, the manager's style should be modified to a greater or lesser extent, deliberately or unthinkingly to suit the circumstances. Management is a flexible commodity and must adapt to different situations. Different managers have different styles of management and the same manager may have a variety of styles depending on different situations. It is clear, that a manager possessing only *one* style of management may be ineffective for the variety of different tasks and people he or she will encounter.

Understanding the management styles open to you will undoubtedly provide you with options, cause you to challenge your assumptions and consequent behaviour and help you to be more effective and efficient leaders in leisure management.

◆ Group dynamics ◆

In earlier times, people recognized that their goals could be accomplished more efficiently when working as part of a group with others who shared the same goal. It is necessary for a manager to understand the dynamics of a group in order to fulfil his or her responsibilities as a group leader.

The study of groups and group dynamics is of paramount importance to the understanding of organizational behaviour for many reasons. In the first place, groups are ubiquitous in our society. Most people belong to several groups, such as a family, a darts team, a church group, or a group at the office [13]. Some may be formally established groups in a commercial or social organization, and others may be more loosely knit associations of people.

The accomplishments of groups are strongly influenced by the behaviour of their individual members and vice versa.

From a managerial perspective, the work group is the primary means by which individual behaviour is co-ordinated to achieve organizational goals. Managers direct the activities of individuals, but they also direct and co-ordinate the interactions within groups. The behaviour of individuals is a primary determinant of the success or failure of a group. As a result, the manager must be aware of individual needs and interpersonal dynamics to manage groups effectively and efficiently.

◆ Reasons for group formation ◆

In order to help individuals accomplish their tasks and to co-ordinate activities to achieve organizational goals, organizations form groups [14]. There are many different reasons why individuals join groups, one of the most important being that members expect affiliation with the group to satisfy a need. These needs can be placed in two categories, internal needs and external needs.

◆ Internal needs ◆

Needs of the individual can be satisfied inside a group in four ways:

- interpersonal attraction
- group activities
- group goals
- satisfaction of the need for affiliation.

Interpersonal attraction is probably the most obvious reason for group formation because people join a group to be with its members. Many factors, however, may influence interpersonal attraction. These include location, physical attraction, perceived ability, similarities in attitudes and beliefs, race, and personality.

A major factor in interpersonal attraction is location, or physical proximity. Very often, people form a group composed of co-workers or neighbours [15]. Proximity may mean nearby desks or offices or neighbouring houses. Location not only provides a setting for interpersonal attraction but can also reinforce it. When people who need to co-ordinate their work have offices close together, informal groups may develop. Group activities can lead to increased interactions and feelings of closeness, and these in turn can result in better working relationships and co-ordination [16]. With opportunities to interact in an informal group, busy executives may be better able to co-ordinate the operations of the organization and thus improve productivity.

Individual needs may also be satisfied in group activities. Consider a group that assembles regularly to play cards, the members may have little interest in who wins or in the intricacies of the game. Social activity such as talking about families, sporting events, and other subjects of mutual interest may be the actual basis of the group.

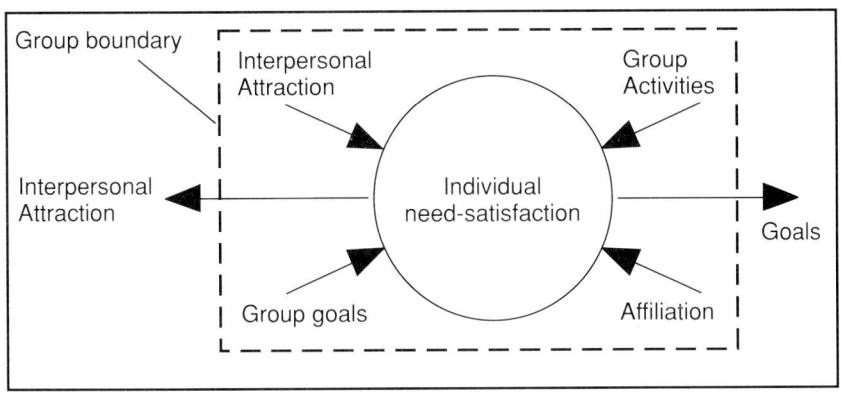

Fig. 5 Sources of need–satisfaction from group membership

Another internal reason for group formation is an identification with group goals that seem to merit a commitment of time and effort. For example, each year in the United States of America thousands of women go door-to-door requesting donations for the 'March of Dimes'. The driving force behind this so-called 'Mothers' March' is the goal of eliminating birth defects. The example illustrates the difference between joining a group because of its activities and joining because of its goals [17]. Many of the women in the 'Mothers' March' may not enjoy the activities of canvassing neighbourhoods and knocking on doors, but their commitment to the goal overrides these personal preferences. This distinction is important in the analysis of individual behaviour in the group.

Lastly, a further internal reason for group formation is satisfaction of the need for affiliation, or companionship [18]. Group membership may be the source of a good deal of personal esteem and provide the foundation for a person's social identity [19]. The group's goals, activities, and location may be largely irrelevant in satisfying the need for affiliation. People who have recently lost a spouse for example, may join groups to replace the companionship they have lost, and care less about the group's purposes or activities.

♦ EXTERNAL NEEDS ♦

Individuals may also join groups to satisfy needs that lie outside the group; either interpersonal attraction to people outside the group, or the pursuit of goals outside the group.

By interpersonal attraction to people outside the group, we mean a person may be able to gain access to certain people only by affiliation with a group. For example, a local property developer wanting to increase his contacts in the area's financial community. Many business leaders, including banking officials, participate in a local association that raises funds for charities and youth groups. The property developer joins the group and takes an active role in its activities, but his main purpose in joining is to gain access to officers of lending institutions.

The pursuit of goals outside the group is exhibited by unions. In general, workers form unions to seek improved salaries and working conditions from employers. These are the reasons for the existence of the union but improved salaries and better working conditions are enjoyed outside the union meetings. The point is that it is possible to join a group to satisfy a need that is separate from the group.

◆ Managing group ◆
Performance in organizations

It is a difficult task managing groups in organizations. The group manager must consider individual motivations for joining the group as well as the group composition. Frequently, a manager can help make sure that the group becomes productive by facilitating its activities in each stage of development. Steps that could be most helpful include the following:

◆ Encouraging open communication and trust among members.

◆ Stimulating discussion of important issues and providing task-relevant information at appropriate times.

◆ Assisting in the analysis of external factors, such as competition, external threats, environmental problems and opportunities.

The manager may employ competition, external threats, goal setting, and participative approaches to harness and channel the productive potential of highly cohesive groups.

Professionals employed in the field of recreation and leisure should be concerned with the provision of staff development opportunities. These include direct counselling, rotation and transfer of employment, guest speakers, supervised readings, audiovisual presentations, staff meetings, panel discussions with key professionals, and the opportunity to observe the leadership style of fellow workers. Workshops ranging from single afternoon sessions to several days' duration can be targeted to such topics as new programme ideas, professional skill development, personal health and maintenance, organizational training and so forth. For instance, a knowledge of time management, brainstorming and problem-solving techniques would enhance the manager's or supervisor's leadership style and would serve as valuable content for in-service training sessions.

♦ WORKING WITH OTHERS: SOME GUIDELINES ♦

If you want to work less and accomplish more, then it is easier to work with people than it is to work against them. As mentioned earlier, in your position as a recreation leader you will probably sometimes experience conflicts with your co-workers. Conflicts with supervisory and peer staff can greatly reduce your chances for achievement and success. Ideally, these conflicts should be resolved by open and honest communication, allowing a positive exchange of ideas and feelings.

LeBoeuf (1979) mentions twelve personalities that disrupt a team approach to getting things done [20]. Do you recognize any of these from work groups of which you have been a part? Do you possess any of these traits?

The critic – comments negatively on every suggestion

The aggressor – contributes unnecessarily hostile comments and questions

The gossip – spreads rumours

The moralist – insists they know what is right and will not tolerate argument

The martyr – accepts extra work and makes sure everyone is aware of the fact

The perfectionist – never achieves anything as continually revising reports, proposals, etc.

The trivia generator – introduces irrelevant and pointless information to important discussion

The short fuse – little control of temper, gets angry quickly and with little justification

The bragger – boasts continually about supposed achievements

The cynic – thinks nothing will ever get done, so no point in trying

The put-down artist – tries to make others feel uncomfortable by making remarks at their expense

The con man – a dishonest liar

LeBoeuf calls these the 'disruptive dozen'. By controlling your own actions however, you can help ensure that the disruptive dozen will have a minimal impact on your own effectiveness. The best way to deal with this dozen is by refusing to become one. The following guidelines are suggestions:

- ♦ Every effort should be made to be an effective communicator. Very often conflicts are created because the persons involved do not fully understand each other.

- ♦ Replace defensiveness with openness. All the disruptive dozen are basically defensive personalities.

- ♦ All criticism should be given in a spirit of kindness, helpfulness, and tact. There will be times when you will be faced with the necessity of pointing out mistakes or constructively commenting on the work of someone else. If handled incorrectly, this can be fertile ground for needless conflict.

◆ Be assertive rather than aggressive. You can resolve conflicts and satisfy your own needs without dominating the other person or clubbing them into submission.

◆ Do not spread rumours about other people, it will not do you any good. It is in your best interest to mind your own business.

◆ It is important to bear in mind that arguing for the sake of arguing is a needless waste of time.

◆ All of us have achievements and possessions that we point to with pride and that mean a good deal to us, do not undermine other people's achievements.

◆ If a major, ongoing, unavoidable conflict is hindering effectiveness, meet it head-on and discuss it honestly with those involved.

◆ Teams and team building ◆

A team is a group of people that can effectively take on any task which it has been set up to do. By effectively, we mean that the quality of the task accomplishment is the best achievable within the time available and makes full and economic use of the resources available to the team. The contribution drawn from each member is of the highest possible quality, and is one which could not have been called into play other than in the context of a supportive team. Dynamic interaction between the individual member and the team exists to such an extent that each continuously adapts to optimize the quality of the team's work. This optimization consists of matching the individual and the team to the progressively developing technical requirements of the task.

This is how a team should work but it is often found that a group of people brought together to form a team do not really blend together and as a result, much valuable time is wasted because tasks are not handled effectively. When many groups in the leisure department, for example, fail to work at peak efficiency, then the effectiveness of the whole department suffers. If groups cannot work effectively by themselves, the probability of relating effectively to other teams with which they have to do business will be reduced.

The manager will very often play a major role in bringing personnel together to form a team. He or she then has to make sure that groups work effectively and collaborate with one another to achieve the task set by the organization or department. The manager's role could be likened to that of the conductor of an orchestra, drawing out from each group and player the best possible quality of performance.

In building up an effective team, two complimentary components are necessary, namely the selection of the members and the training of the team. Training starts with some kind of instruction so that members know what is expected of them. Then later they practise and repeatedly review their own progress, so eventually they become proficient at any new skills required. Collaboration between teams can also be improved through practice and review, provided a process for developing effectiveness is at work throughout the organization or department.

Even though in industry team-building training has been systematically pursued along these lines over the past 25 years, it is only lately that the selection of team members has got much beyond the point of intuitive judgement.

Research has shown that the mix of personal characteristics in members of a team is a major determinant of the team's success. Very often it is not simply the technical expertise that the members bring, for this can be of second-order importance, but it is the way they interact.

There are many successful methods of building teams. Teams are an essential part of all efficient organizations, especially those which are changing rapidly, and managers should encourage the formation of more teams such as task groups and working parties, to foster innovation and the effective management of change. All local authorities operate with a top management team, which is an obvious place to start trying to improve effectiveness. Do not assume however, that all managerial activity should be a team activity. It is not necessary for routine work needing little co-ordination but it is necessary for solving complex problems in conditions of high uncertainty.

◆ THE SYSTEMATIC APPROACH ◆

All teams should be trained by encouraging them to follow a systematic approach. Certain individuals who possess the talent and skill to solve problems intuitively may not like following a systematic approach. The intuitive thinker tends to solve a problem by devising solutions and testing them until such time as he or she is satisfied with the quality of his or her decision. However, most individuals are more effective when their thought-processes and actions are systematic; and even an intuitive thinker sometimes meets situations in which he or she needs a systematic approach.

A commonly understood systematic approach becomes essential when people are working in groups since an intuitive approach cannot be followed and understood by other members of the group. A simple systematic approach provides a foundation for teamwork, and a basis from which to develop ways of tackling problems. It consists of a logical series of steps that are followed in order to achieve a given task or deal with a particular problem. (Similar to the effective decision-making procedures pp. (14–15).

All systematic approaches emphasize the importance of the team defining and agreeing its objectives for no team can work effectively unless everyone in it knows where it is going. Soundly framed objectives are as specific, concise, time-bound and as observable or measurable as possible. They tend to be quantitative rather than qualitative, results-centred rather than activity-centred and realistic rather than pessimistic.

Objectives can be broadened by asking the question 'In order to achieve what?' and can be narrowed down by asking 'What has to be achieved to attain this?' Objectives that appear vague and woolly should be omitted.

Teams sometimes invite an outsider to be a consultant to the group and to coach it in improving effectiveness. A consultant, such as an industrial trainer, or university recreation lecturer, experienced in group processes, can bring a useful amount of objectivity and detachment into the proceedings, and enable the team to face issues that left to itself, it would probably suppress.

◆ Conclusion ◆

An understanding of teamwork and team building are essential requirements for any manager in either a leisure or a general business setting.

The key to effective and successful leisure management is the ability to get results from other people, through, and in conjunction with, other people. Management is about people not systems: people coming together to achieve the clear objectives of their organization. In a very real way you, as a manager, have a contract with your organization: everyday you give something of your life and receive something in return; not only a salary but a genuine chance to achieve. At the end of the day you and your subordinates should derive some meaning which reinforces and reaffirms your own values. Guidelines in this chapter have been given to help you achieve this difficult aim. In addition, the knowledge gained will enable you to approach your responsibilities with greater insight, creativity and vision. You should also have gained some additional knowledge about leadership and group dynamics which will enable you to lead your team more successfully in an exciting, changing, yet extremely demanding working environment. The success of a leisure department or organization will always depend on both the people within it and also, importantly, on the effectiveness of its leader or manager.

DISCUSSION QUESTIONS

1. What traits do you think characterize successful leaders/managers within the leisure management field?
2. Why is the effectiveness or ability of the Leisure Manager so crucial to the programme success?
3. The Recreation Manager has different levels of staff. Many staff work long unsocial hours and undertake various types of work. You have just been appointed the new Recreation Manager. Describe your leadership style as the newly appointed manager taking on board the issues described above.
4. Discuss the provision of staff development opportunities for the leisure employee.
5. The Leisure Manager's role could be likened to that of the conductor of an orchestra, drawing out from each group and player the best possible quality of performance. Give your views on this statement.

◆ Case study ◆

Mr. George Black had declared his intention to retire at the end of the current year. He had served as the Leisure Centre Manager for over 15 years, and whenever others thought of the Centre they naturally thought of him. Although somewhat of an autocrat, he was not unapproachable. This, together with a deference to his age and experience, had led the staff, particularly the senior members, to work effectively under him.

The Chief Leisure Officer, a democratic administrator, along with other senior members of the Leisure Department short-listed two candidates both from within Mr. George Black's Leisure Centre.

The first candidate, Mr. Robert Gibson, was a strong domineering individual who had been in the Leisure Centre for ten years and was highly regarded by one and all. The other candidate, Mr. John Davies, was a rather unassuming man. Although he had less experience (2 years) than Mr. Gibson, he had the ability to get people to work together as a team, and he had a degree in Leisure Management.

Both candidates were interviewed and the Chief Leisure officer now wished to select the new Leisure Centre Manager.

1. What are the central issues in this case?

2. What guiding principles are involved?

3. Who would you recommend for the post and why?

LEISURE MARKETING: THE MARKETING MIX

*L*eisure Managers are becoming increasingly involved in marketing their products or services. Marketing, for Leisure Managers, is primarily concerned with the development of strategies, policies and operations — usually on a competitive standing. All forms of marketing, in terms of implementation and strategy, rely heavily on political and economic circumstances. These will determine the extent of production (supply) and consumption (demand), and influence the prevailing level of competition. Furthermore, a marketing strategy, or plan, will provide Leisure Managers with a philosophy of management, a sense of direction and the ability to respond to the requirements of consumers.

An increasing demand is made on Leisure Managers to generate income and thus to maximize profits. This is especially important to those employed in the private sector. In order to make a profit, leisure agencies must offer products and/or services that are needed and wanted by customers or consumers. There must be a demand for the leisure products and/or services being provided and this is where marketing plays a vital role.

Ideally, marketing involves utilizing an organization's resources to satisfy customer needs, the understanding and practical application of various skills and discovering the significance of marketing in everyday activities. Successful marketing will supply potential consumers with information explaining how an organization can satisfy their needs. Some of these potential consumers will go on to buy the goods manufactured by the organization, or to use the services it offers. Thus profits will be increased. One may attempt to describe marketing as all about attracting, satisfying and keeping hold of customers, whether the industry is concerned with producing goods or providing a service. Leisure agencies provide services. Most people regard marketing as synonymous with selling or advertising. However, these are only parts of the story, for marketing involves numerous activities and skills. It includes consumer analysis, market research, product development, buying and pricing, distribution and promotion.

Authors have put forward varying definitions of marketing and the variety has led to confusion. Some consider marketing to be a business-orientated activity involving selling, advertising and distributing products; whilst others understand marketing in much broader terms, such as, 'those activities which direct the flow of goods and services from production to consumption' [21]. [Alexander (1960).]

Stanton (1975), focusing on customer satisfaction, offered a broad definition of marketing as a 'total system of interacting business activities designed to plan, price, promote and distribute want-satisfying goods and services to present and potential customers' [22].

Stanton highlights two major concepts: (a) systems and (b) want-satisfying goods and services. Marketing is seen as a system, with interacting and interdependent parts functioning as a unified whole. Parts of the system may include pricing, promotion and planning, all being inter-related, interactive and interdependent. The other concept of satisfying wants is also fundamental to marketing because it is the customer who determines the products or services to be produced and marketed, not the producers or manufacturers.

Kotler (1983) uses the concept of exchange in defining marketing. Exchange involves two or more parties, each possessing something desired by the other(s), voluntarily agreeing to enter into a trading relationship which is mutually satisfactory. Kotler regards marketing as the, 'human activity directed at satisfying needs and wants through exchange processes'. He also stresses the point of, 'getting the right goods to the right people at the right place at the right time and at the right price' [23].

People involved in leisure marketing should attempt to:

◆ identify the needs and desires of consumers of leisure products and services,
◆ provide information about new and improved products and services,
◆ inform customers and consumers about the many diverse products and services available,
◆ determine appropriate prices,
◆ place the products and services where they are needed and wanted.

These points are far from comprehensive but do indicate the range of marketing activities.

Leisure, in all its contexts, is the largest single industry employing the greatest national percentage of the total workforce, and it is still growing! Inevitably, a level of competition exists between the various leisure and recreation agencies which operate. Therefore, today's Leisure Manager has to employ competitive marketing strategies. For any leisure agency or company wishing to enjoy longevity, its management must respond to competition with creative and innovative action so that a competitive superiority prevails. The striving and determination for market leadership on the part of leisure companies is the driving force in a competitive market system. Marketing may be regarded as maintaining a profitable market leadership by responding to buyer's needs and wants.

To summarize, for the purpose of Leisure Managers, marketing can be described as co-ordinated systems of business activities designed specifically to provide products and services that satisfy the needs and wants of customers through an exchange process.

◆ Marketing mix ◆

Typically, marketing is concerned with the manipulation of four major variables. These are:

- **Product** and/or service to be offered.
- **Price** at which they should be sold or charged.
- **Place** in terms of the location or venue, where the product or service is manufactured or offered, plus the distribution systems by which goods and services are conveyed to places where they can be purchased by the consumer.
- **Promotion** or how the products or services should be promoted or exposed.

These four 'P's' when considered together are referred to as the 'marketing mix' and they will now be discussed at some length. Although the four 'P's' are very broad variables, marketing has become very complex, so one can add further 'P's' to create a more flexible matrix. (See p. 60.)

◆ Product ◆

A product (or service) is something that is capable of satisfying people's needs or wants. In a commercial context, a product is viewed as the complete package, or value, a company or leisure agency has to offer to its customers to satisfy their needs.

Companies devote much time and cost to producing the products that customers require. Nowadays customers require more than just the product, they also require service. For example, information technology has become an important force in all types of business management, and a customer may want a computer to help manage his or her business affairs. A computer is a tangible item offered to satisfy the customer's needs. However, most customers' needs go beyond physically owning a computer. The customer will, in this case, have a need for related services, perhaps in financing the purchase of the computer or back-up services for repairs. Other customers may want advice on the use of the computer and all its innovative features.

A service according to Kotler (1983) is

> *'any activity or benefit that one party can offer to another that is essentially intangible and does not result in the ownership of anything. Its production may or may not be tied to a physical product'* [23].

This is most appropriate to the leisure industry in that it does provide a 'service' for its customers or users in certain sectors.

Since leisure is very diverse, it provides a host of products and services, mostly dependent on three major sectors:

The public sector	The private sector	The voluntary sector
Sports and leisure centres, parks, playgrounds, museums, libraries, theatres, public halls, community centres, swimming pools and tourist information centres.	Health clubs, discotheques, leisure pools, theme parks, cinemas, hotels and restaurants, tourist attractions and amusement centres.	Play schemes, sports grounds, community activities, clubs and societies and conservation work.

The above outlines the scope of leisure. Each sector provides different products or activities and customers will require different services from each.

◆ PRODUCT PLANNING ◆

Major activities associated with the product element of the marketing mix include product planning and development, packaging, standardization, grading and buying. Product planning and development are primarily concerned with identifying, creating and modifying products or services to meet the needs and wants of customers.

***P**lanning a product* or service is a complex and challenging task. Product planning is the first major task of the marketing manager and involves several stages. Consider the case of someone wishing to set up a company to manufacture track suits, he or she must:

◆ Identify a product that meets the demands, needs and wants of customers.

- Identify customers' basic needs — for warmth and protection both in cold weather and after participation in the game.
- Think about physical features, the texture of the material, colour, style and quality.
- Think about backup service — can replacement be guaranteed if the wrong size is supplied?
- Bear in mind psychological features. Does the track suit feel good? Is it comfortable? Does it allow relaxation and freedom of movement?
- Examine the total product — is the price satisfactory and does the product meet expectations?

If these stages are followed, product planning can be seen to have three basic components, consideration of basic benefits, physical features and related services designed to satisfy the needs of the leisure market. It is always worth remembering that a market is made up of people with the purchasing power and the willingness to buy specific products and services.

Packaging, if used, must meet certain requirements such as: appropriate size and strength, strong visual appeal and the ability to withstand physical distribution or transportation.

Standardization is also important, it involves establishing basic measures or limits to which products or services must consistently conform. Sports equipment must meet certain standards, as must swimming pool maintenance and the condition of sports centre buildings.

Grading refers to the act of determining whether the standard has been met and, if it has been met, to what level. Grading is usually a measure of superiority and an example is the one to four-star rating of hotels, restaurants and garages.

Patterns of consumer behaviour also play an important role in product development. If the people involved in product development know who is buying their product and why, then they can respond to changes in consumer demand.

◆ PRODUCT MIX ◆

In most cases a leisure agency or company offers more than one product or service to its customers; some offer over a hundred, such as amusement parks. The combination of products and services offered by a leisure company is referred to as the product mix.

The product mix is achieved by putting together a number of closely related products having a similar function, these are called product lines. When a product mix is marketed, its width, depth and consistency need careful consideration. Product width is the number of different lines offered whilst product depth is the number of items or brands in the total mix, or the number of items in a line. Good product depth would ensure a customer had a wide choice of colours, brands, prices, styles and sizes to match their needs when choosing a track suit, for example. Product consistency is the relationship of product lines and items in terms of final, or total, benefits to the customer. Consistency is achieved if a customer can purchase a complete matching outfit of clothing in one store, or if all the tools and materials needed to complete a job can be purchased under one roof.

Sometimes it is best to have only a few product lines. For example, if a leisure marketer attempts to serve a number of distinctly identifiable markets with a wide assortment of products the sales force may be unable to target its activities effectively thus the sales effort may be diluted. Conversely, if the product line is too narrow, customer needs may not be effectively met because choice is limited.

◆ Product life cycle ◆

Markets very rarely remain static. Over time, some products will cease to generate benefits or profits. Therefore, Leisure Managers have to look to new products. Customers' needs are always changing, hence new or modified products need to be introduced to meet those needs as they occur. Changing trends cause products to move in a cyclical fashion and the stages that a product passes through from introduction to removal from the market are referred to as the product life cycle.

If a new product is introduced and accepted by a market segment, it enjoys a degree of unique advantage. However, if the market segment has potential, the product will be copied or slightly modified by other producers. As time goes on and more companies market a similar product, the original product's distinctiveness is reduced. Therefore, the instigator of the original product will lose some of the initial competitive advantage. With continued passage of time customer needs may change to such an extent that the product no longer merits being kept in the product mix.

We will now look more closely at the product life cycle. During its competitive phase, a product may go through five distinct stages: Introduction, Acceptance, Turbulence, Saturation and Decline.

- ◆ Introduction – a new product is introduced. The product may perform an old task in a new way or do something not previously possible. The characteristics of this stage are: slow increase in sales, few competitors, high prices, high production and marketing costs, limited distribution and frequent product modifications.

- ◆ Acceptance – widespread buyer approval is secured for the product. Acceptance has the following characteristics: price adjustments, rapid rise in sales, increase in the number of direct competitors, greater demands

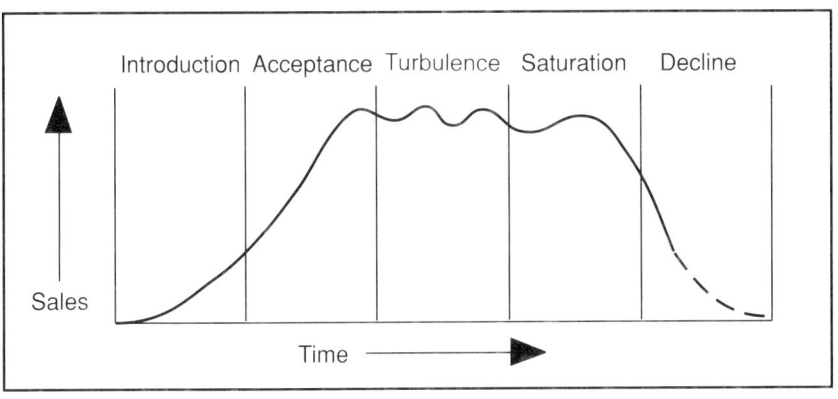

Fig. 6 The product life cycle showing the traditional stages and pattern through which a product passes.

for distribution outlets and improved line–production methods.

♦ Turbulence – a period of extreme competitive volatility characterized by the following; the rate of market growth levels out, changes in product and service policy occur, profits fall, trade-ins appear, the price of the product falls and parts and maintenance requirements increase.

♦ Saturation – replacement sales dominate the total volume of sales because those who previously purchased the product are now purchasing a new one. An example is the purchasing of a new car with additional accessories to replace the old one. Characteristics of saturation are: trade-ins dominate the market, sales rise and fall with basic economic forces, it is necessary to make costs competitive for survival and the number of competitors stabilize.

♦ Decline – new innovations by competitors may make the product obsolete, hence a decline in sales and profit rapidly occur. Other causes of decline may be changes in people's purchasing habits, attitudes and values. At this stage a new product is required to restore confidence and survival.

Some products may go through the cycle quicker than others. Some may not complete the cycle at all because they do not gain acceptance. All leisure marketers should understand the concept of product life cycle for it will serve as a means of analysing sales, profits, competitors, customers' needs, marketing strategies and management decisions.

It is clear from the above that a decision about which product or service to offer a customer involves careful consideration of many salient points. Leisure marketing, in terms of product development, is becoming a prominent feature and an essential requirement among Leisure Managers for the industry is continuing to expand at a rapid rate. Once the product has been developed, managers move on to another major 'P' of the marketing mix, that of Price.

♦ Price ♦

Price is an important concept for both the buyer and seller. The price of a product is simply the amount of money for which anything is sold, bought or offered for sale, it is the amount a customer is willing to pay.

The pricing of a product is difficult and complex, for many considerations need to be taken into account. There are no more important decisions in marketing affairs than those connected with pricing. Improper pricing of a product may nullify the effect of all other business actions.

If a product is over-priced, then it may be priced out of the market because customers will shop elsewhere. Similarly, if a product is too low in price, customers become dubious about its quality and reliability and go elsewhere. To overcome these problems, prices tend to move towards an average; all leading competitors become aware of each other's prices and so variations in price between products are small.

Another major influence that price has is in determining how profitable any product or service can be. The subject of profits will be discussed later in this section. Having established some important roles that price plays in the marketing process, some thought must be given to the factors which may help leisure marketers to determine the price of their products or services.

♦ Factors affecting price ♦

The price that is paid for a product or service is influenced by a number of factors such as quality, delivery terms, premiums, discounts, credit or financial schemes for payment for the product or service being offered. In addition, pricing policy may be influenced by wider political considerations such as the level of interest rates, energy supplies, competition from foreign suppliers, high unemployment, and legal requirements for stricter safety measures. Additional factors may include technological advances, pressures to make profits, and changes in supply and demand.

Virtually all leisure industries have pricing objectives. These may include maximizing sales and profits, meeting target sales, attaining a target share of the available market, making a certain return on investments and setting a competitive price. It is evident that pricing plays a very important role in the marketing strategy of a leisure company.

Products and services may vary in price due to off peak periods, seasonal trends, quantity discounts, reduced rates for different age groups, private or commercial use of a facility or product, and geographical variations. Prices do not have to be rigidly fixed at all times, they may fluctuate in the instances cited above so that resources and products continue to be used and sold.

To conclude this section the following list may help leisure marketers and managers to establish a strategy in developing the price of a product or service they offer.

- ◆ Determine price objectives.
- ◆ Determine an estimated unit cost of the product.
- ◆ Estimate demand by employing market research techniques.
- ◆ Study and analyse competing products in terms of their quantity, quality and price.
- ◆ Devise a pricing strategy in terms of cost-orientation, discount and variations which might occur during the product's life cycle.
- ◆ Set a competitive price.

◆ PLACE ◆

Place refers to the location or venue from which a leisure business operates. Location is an important consideration for all business enterprises. The products and services offered must be sited for customer convenience, taking into account ease of access, parking facilities and prominent frontage of the premises. Whatever leisure pursuit is offered, it must be sited in a suitable place so that the attention of potential consumers can be attracted. Groups with special needs, such as the disabled, the elderly, and mothers with young children must not be forgotten, they are important potential consumers and attention must be paid to making the sports centre accessible to them. When thinking about place, one must also check the location of similar businesses. It might prove advantageous to be near a similar business, or it might prove fatal. If an existing business is in operation and is very successful it might be best to venture elsewhere. On the other hand, if the other business is weak you could attract its dissatisfied customers.

Many businesses have collapsed purely because they set up in the wrong place. Therefore, great care must be given to location, especially because the initial outlay can be huge. It is important to be sure to have your products and services available in the right place at the right time. Customers depend on their wants and needs being satisfied in a suitable and convenient place. Successful leisure marketing takes place when the entire workforce contribute to letting their customers have the right products and services at the right price at the right time and in the right place.

Very often, place is understood as a point for distribution of products and services, but this will be discussed during the section on physical distribution.

◆ Promotion ◆

Promotion is another vital element in the marketing mix. It can be regarded as the means of communicating information from the providers of leisure services to the buyers or customers. Its aim is to inform prospective customers that a leisure business has the right product and services available in the right place and at the right price.

Most promotional activities can be classified as one of the following: advertising, selling, public relations, publicity and sales promotion. Communication can take many forms, written, verbal or audio-visual.

The important point is that information is put across concisely and coherently. It must be to the point to encourage people to spread the news of the product or service to others.

There are, however, certain barriers to communication, causing the information or intended message to become distorted or ineffective. Such barriers may be classified into three broad areas:

- Physical, or environmental, barriers — for example, background noise, failure of communication equipment, or sheer distance.
- Psychological barriers — these may stem from personality conflicts, differences in opinions or reluctance to give full details for fear of upsetting one's superior or customer.
- Linguistic barriers — these occur when words or symbols have more than one interpretation or are loosely defined. Words such as; young, old, good, poor, small, and large can be understood differently, especially when no comparison is offered. Therefore, it is vital that more specific words are used or some scale given to clarify the meaning of such words.

'**P**romotion', in a marketing context, refers to various ways of communicating. All forms of promotion should be customer-orientated as it is the customer who buys the product or service. Promotional material must contain persuasive messages aimed at the intended customer. Regardless of the method used to convey the promotion message, three major factors should be given careful consideration:

- The message should be designed and delivered in such a way that it will gain the attention of the intended audience.
- To ensure the message is transmitted effectively, words and symbols should only be used if they will be understood by the receiver in the way intended by the sender.

♦ The messages should highlight needs and wants and indicate ways that these may be satisfied, by buying or using the product or service on offer.

♦ PROMOTION AND THE PRODUCT LIFE CYCLE ♦

The cycle of promotion follows the product life cycle (see p. 46). During the introductory stage in a product's life cycle prospective customers may not be aware that they need or want the product. It is vital that customers are told that the product exists, how they can benefit from owning it and what it can do.

This can be achieved through promotional campaigns, and, importantly, through attending trade exhibitions or shows. Trade shows provide a chance to demonstrate the new product to retailers.

Following on from the introductory stage, greater emphasis is placed on advertising, which will be discussed in detail later on. Basically, the seller, or provider, must stimulate demand and point out the unique benefits the product or service offers, and in some cases explain how it is better than other leading brands or competitors. If this is accomplished successfully, greater acceptance will be achieved.

During the turbulence and saturation stages of the product cycle, the product generally faces stiffest competition, therefore, various persuasive techniques need to be applied with vigorous advertising.

Ultimately the product will reach the stage of decline where demand falls or the product needs updating owing to technological advances. Certainly, some products have longer life cycles than others but will eventually decline because of economic or cultural influences. During the decline stage, promotional efforts are reduced and greater concentration given to new or substitute products entering the market.

♦ THE PROMOTIONAL BUDGET ♦

All forms of promotional activity are expensive, but all businesses must set some form of promotional budget. Leading multinational companies spend millions of pounds or dollars to promote, advertise and sell their products but smaller businesses have more limited funds set aside for promotion. A major problem for managers is to decide how much money should be spent on promotional activities.

The promotional budget will essentially depend on the company's economic condition, the activity of competitors and the cost of promotional materials and media. Budgets are generally projected on the basis of past or anticipated sales or profits, bearing in mind what competitors are spending on promotion and what it costs to achieve objectives. Some companies do not set aside a predetermined sum for promotion, but simply use whatever funds are available, whereas others set aside a proportion of their profit.

Budgets related to sales or profits are usually calculated as a percentage applied to one of the following bases: past sales, anticipated sales, past profits, anticipated profits, number of units or product items sold in the past and, the number of units expected to be sold in the future.

Whichever of these bases is used to determine the amount of money to be spent on promotional activities, it is vital that managers remember that promotion leads to sales, and hence to profits. Economic conditions will have influenced past sales and profits and may influence future sales. However, if a company performed poorly because of poor economic conditions, a promotion budget tied to past performance may prove inadequate as economic conditions improve.

It is wise to monitor competitors' promotional activities, but not to base one's own promotional budget on what competitors are doing. Some competitors may be making poor decisions, therefore, one's own business should not copy their tactics. A company adopting promotional objectives should clearly outline those objectives. This forces the marketing manager to define the goals of the promotional programme, making the planning more realistic and accountable. Planned, detailed expenditure can be more easily justified than spontaneous expenditure. Furthermore, management should periodically review expenditure against progress made towards the achievement of objectives.

The objectives method is useful, but promotional budgets should not be restricted to a cast of concrete. Occasionally the promotional budget should be reviewed and necessary adjustments should be made. Economic conditions, increased competition and a host of other variables may render objectives obsolete or create the need to set new objectives. Flexibility is vital to strengthen the overall promotional programme.

◆ A SUGGESTED TEN POINT ◆
SUCCESSFUL PROMOTION PROGRAMME

- ◆ *Good planning and preparation* — The successful promotion of a product or service requires careful planning and preparation.
- ◆ *Define realistic objectives* — Ideally objectives must be defined so that

they are relatively easy to measure when the promotional activities are completed, making evaluation simple.

◆ *Co-ordination* — Since promotion involves numerous tasks and may include several specialist people, a means of co-ordinating all these activities needs to be acquired to reduce unnecessary expense or duplication of work and to produce a smooth, synchronized chain of events.

◆ *Target audience* — Efforts must always be focused on the sector the product is aimed at. Do not lose sight of this.

◆ *Good management support* — If promotional activities are to be effective, then support must be given and shown by senior management.

◆ *Good channel support* — Many promotional activities will depend heavily on other people or middlemen in the distribution of promotional materials. The support of middlemen is vital.

◆ *Good timekeeping* — This supplements good planning and preparation. If a promotional programme is to be implemented as planned, good timekeeping and punctuality are necessary prerequisites.

◆ *Creative ideas* — Repetition, dull presentation and poor quality material may have a damaging effect rather than putting over a favourable, likeable and beneficial impression of the product or service.

◆ *An adequate and well-trained sales staff* — Good promotion depends heavily on well-trained sales staff. Training seminars may be held so that sales staff can be briefed about the products and all parts of the promotional programme.

◆ *Adequate advertising* — Advertising is a very powerful tool of communication. Adverts can be targeted to reach a specific audience and they can be placed in a variety of media — press, radio or television. They attract interest, arouse curiosity and possibly cause consumers to develop desires for a particular product.

◆ Promotion: public relations ◆

Public relations (PR) also play a vital role in the promotional programme of a company, regardless of size. PR relates to activities designed to earn public understanding, respect and acceptance and to create or project a favourable image of the company. The 'public' are all those individuals, groups or companies a PR department interacts with, or hopes to influence. Marketing becomes that much easier if a company has good public relations. Sometimes the initials 'PR' are used to stand for 'performance' and 'recognition', not 'public relations'. All companies strive to achieve good performance and recognition.

◆ Promotion: selling ◆

Selling features prominently in the promotional aspect of the marketing mix. Selling consists of individuals using persuasive communication techniques aimed at helping the prospective customer choose a product or service to satisfy their need or want.

Selling is an art requiring training and practice. We have all been confronted by salesmen; sometimes we buy, sometimes we go elsewhere and sometimes we purchase an alternative product. The salesman's manner is vital. Some sales people are good, others too pushy whilst others know nothing, or very little, about the product being sold.

It is well worth a company having a well trained sales staff and ensuring that each member of the sales team is well informed about the product or service being offered. After all, it is the selling of the product that generates the revenue needed to pay expenses and to yield profits.

◆ Promotion: advertising ◆

Advertising is an important method of communication and its main purpose is to sell a product. It is marketing's most visible form of communication.

Whilst advertising is costly, it does help to keep the price of a product or service lower. Without sales messages being directed to prospective purchases, fewer products would be sold and prices would be higher. The greater the rate of turnover, the lower the price because increased sales lead to decreased production costs and this decrease can be passed on to the public. But, a high turnover will only result from effective advertising and other promotional activities. Classical examples are the sale of calculators, video cassette recorders and digital watches. When these products originally appeared on the market they were relatively expensive, but since advertising made them popular, production costs and overheads fell and so did prices.

The initial task of advertising is to tell people that a product or service is available and to inform them about the benefits that can be derived from owning or using it. The advertising message must be truthful and informative. An advertisement need not only put across messages regarding a product or service, but also reinforce corporate identity and help generate goodwill to the company. It is very important to foster goodwill and maintain the reputation of a company in addition to telling people about its products and services.

◆ Targeting the advertising message ◆

It is important for the marketing manager to specify target markets which those planning the advertising must try to reach. The target market may be car owners, the unemployed, pensioners or children. Once the target market has been established, the appropriate media can be chosen so that the message is seen, heard or read by target customers.

Matching appropriate media to target customers is important. Those selling advertising space engage in market research to develop profiles of the people who subscribe to their publications or listen to or view their programmes. The result of such research is demographic data concerning the age range, affluence, gender and geographical distribution of their readership or audience. Information is also available about the number of people who watch a given TV programme, buy a particular magazine or listen to local radio.

In spite of such detailed information, the media providers cannot be definite about who actually reads a specific page or sees or hears a specific programme.

Most providers of products and services advertise through specialized trade journals. There are now many leisure and recreation magazines and journals, these have extensive sections for advertisements. Both national and local advertising can enhance the chance of reaching specific target groups and chances can be further improved by careful planning of the position or timing of an advertisement or commercial.

◆ Examples ◆

- ◆ The owner of a health salon placed a commercial on the local radio, specifying that it should be heard both before and following the daily exercise programme.
- ◆ An owner of a travel agency frequently advertises in a Sunday newspaper and specifies that her adverts should appear in the travel section.
- ◆ A major leisure company advertises their product on television and specifies that adverts appear after football, basketball and hockey programmes.

In each of the examples, the placement or position and the timing were chosen to direct the advertising message to specific target groups.

However, selecting the appropriate medium, time and position of an advertisement are not the only requirements. A further consideration needs to be taken into account if an advertisement is to succeed, and this can be achieved by applying the A.I.D.A. principle.

◆ THE A.I.D.A. PRINCIPLE ◆

A.I.D.A. stands for 'Attention', 'Interest', 'Desire' and 'Action'. The *attention* of a customer must be retained throughout any communication. *Interest* is developed by telling a customer the benefits they can derive from a product and also by employing the USP principle (Unique Selling Proposition), i.e. telling the customer the benefits and advantages you offer over your competitors. *Desire* concerns the ability to stimulate your customer to want what is offered, and *Action* occurs when a customer purchases or uses a specific facility. Essentially, A.I.D.A. means 'grab *Attention*, create *Interest*, arouse *Desire* and get *Action*'. The various components of A.I.D.A. are explained more fully below.

◆ ATTENTION ◆

An advertisement must attract attention long enough to leave an impression. Few people study the host of advertisements that consumers are constantly bombarded with unless they are looking for something specific. An advertisement may attempt to capture attention through using a bold headline, an attractive illustration, a cartoon character, a celebrity presenter or similar device.

If too much humour is used this may distract from the seriousness of the message. Controversial or shocking headlines may create negative attitudes. Illustrations that do not really relate to the message may give the impression that the message is false. Whilst every attempt must be made to capture attention, adverts must be accurate and truthful.

◆ INTEREST ◆

Holding interest is always a difficult task but whatever policy is used, the advert must relate to the product or service and to the customer. Illustrations and language must be compatible with the experiences and attitudes of target customers. Layout, presentation and colouring all play their role in making an advertisement attractive, interesting and eye catching.

◆ DESIRE ◆

To cause target customers to want a specific product is again a difficult task. The advertiser must try and get some idea of how the target customers think, behave and make decisions so that he or she can try to justify the product. Slogans are often used to provoke emotion, or to suggest that a product is associated with some generally desired end which can be achieved by buying the product.

◆ Action ◆

All advertising is aimed at provoking immediate or future buying. For example the following tactics are used to motivate customers to act quickly in order to take advantage of special offers or circumstances.

- ◆ Sale starts Monday at 09.00 am.
- ◆ Reduced membership fees for first 100 members.
- ◆ Vouchers valid until 31st August.
- ◆ Closing down – all products must be sold.
- ◆ Free gift if order received by 1st May.

Not all advertisements are designed to provoke prompt sales. Some campaigns are progressive. Early in the campaign adverts may be used as a means of persuading potential consumers to accept a new idea. Later adverts will try to move the customer towards a purchase decision and ultimately to action, that is, buying the product.

◆ Selecting the appropriate media ◆

Leisure marketers have a vast choice of media and must determine which is the best suited to reach the greatest number of target customers with the greatest impact and at the lowest cost. The characteristics of each advertising medium should be examined carefully before a firm decision is made, and examples are discussed below.

◆ Printed media ◆

This includes newspapers, magazines, direct mail and entertainment guides. Each of these has advantages and limitations, which need to be considered before making a final decision.

- ◆ *Newspapers*
  Newspapers contain advertisements for virtually all types of businesses. They can carry messages both nationally and locally and adverts appear as displays or in the classified section. Display adverts are usually large and contain persuasive messages. Classified advertisements are small, consisting of only a few lines. They simply announce that certain goods or services are for sale. Many newspapers can produce coloured advertisements for an additional charge. You can usually specify when and where your advert is to appear. You will be able to choose whether to draw up the advertisement yourself, or

whether to have this done by either the newspaper publishers or an advertising agency. The drawbacks of newspaper advertising are threefold; short life — newspapers become stale quickly, and are generally thrown away the following day, so the chance of the impact of an advert carrying over the date of publication is minimal; hasty reading — people rarely read every word in their newspaper, so the advertisement could quite easily be overlooked entirely; poor reproduction — the quality of reproduction in newspapers is often quite poor so the impact of an attractive advert will be blunted.

◆ *Magazines*
Magazines can be used to reach a national consumer market or members of a specialized trade or industry. There are a host of leisure, sporting and recreational magazines on the market. Unlike newspapers, magazines are generally kept at home, in waiting rooms, libraries and reception areas for relatively long periods of time. As a result, a magazine advertisement may be seen and read more frequently than a newspaper advertisement. Also, magazines are generally printed on high-quality paper so that excellent reproduction in black and white or colour is possible. However, an advertisement must be prepared well in advance and little chance for alterations occurs once it has been submitted.

◆ *Direct mail*
Direct mail is another means of reaching a large audience. The growth and proliferation of direct mail has created a degree of resentment amongst many consumers who refer to such mail as 'junk mail'. Nevertheless, this system still prevails in the hope of keeping specific products alive, maintaining sales and eliminating the use of salespersons. Forms of direct mail include brochures, post cards, catalogues, leaflets, folders and booklets. The advantages of direct mailing are that it can be directed at a precise target audience and can take advantage of seasonal trends. Major disadvantages are cost and the possibility of the recipient throwing the advertising material away immediately.

◆ *Mail shots*
Mail shots are single sided sheets used to advertise products, services, ideas or events. They can be used for posters and displayed in prominent places where they can be seen. Mail shots are used in sports centres where they are displayed on noticeboards highlighting special events and other relevant information.

◆ *Entertainment guides*
Entertainment guides are published for circulation in large cities or places that offer a high level of entertainment. Restaurants, hotels,

theatres, museums, art galleries, night-clubs and other companies that cater for leisure for visitors may find a local entertainment guide useful for advertising their products and services.

◆ Broadcast media ◆

The high costs involved in this form of advertising normally restrict the users to well-established companies.

- *Radio*
  A radio's mobility provides much flexibility for an advertiser. It can be heard in a variety of locations. Radio advertisements are usually allocated a time span of 30 seconds, one minute or longer. The advertiser can choose the regularity and timing of the broadcast most suited to the target audience, for example sports fans, business people, entertainers or do-it-yourself enthusiasts. Furthermore, there are a variety of stations and programmes throughout the country that attract certain groups of listeners. Radio, like all forms of media, has its limitations. Radio stations face vigorous competition for listeners from competing stations, television, newspapers and other forms of media. A further limitation of radio advertising is that, unlike printed advertising, messages pass relatively quickly and are not available for review or immediate repeat.

- *Television*
  The cost of television advertising is very high, especially during peak viewing times. However, when the size and variety of the audience together with the level of impact are measured against the cost of the advertisement, the overall expenditure per head is relatively low. Like radio, television can repeat messages frequently, according to the advertiser's budget.
  Television provides a medium that can demonstrate a product, create a mood, make an intensive sales pitch or establish a slogan, but there are shortcomings. Words in print tend to have a more lasting impression than unwritten messages. Printed words carry a stamp of authenticity that broadcasting cannot attain. Another limitation of television advertising is in its 'mortality' rate. Many viewers may switch channels during the commercials or leave the room, meanwhile they have not seen or heard the advertisements. Additionally, a popular programme on another channel may attract much of the potential audience that an advertiser hopes to reach.

◆ Other media ◆

Other forms of media do exist but are difficult to classify.

- *Outdoor media* include the large standardized signs strategically placed in High streets or in prominent places, for example around football pitches. Non-standardized posters may be displayed on other premises where space is rented. The advantages of outdoor media advertising are that the messages are simple and easy to comprehend; repetition is a built-in factor because people may pass an advertisement several times, and it is a cost-effective method of reaching a large number of consumers. Limitations include a limit to how much can be displayed. Legal requirements exist in the placement of outdoor advertising to prevent accidents or congestion caused by possible distraction.

- *Transit advertising* consists of messages placed on the exterior of public transport vehicles or commecial vans. Small posters are also displayed in subways, railway and bus terminals. Advertising on the interior of trains and buses, for instance, has a great impact on passengers who have time to read and digest the advertisements.

- *Speciality advertising* refers to the giving of small inexpensive items, for example, a ball-point pen bearing a company's name and address, and a short message, or slogan, to a preselected audience. The item should be of good and durable quality, so that it is used over a long period and provides a constant reminder of the advertiser.

◆ Subsidiary P's for the marketing mix ◆

The four major components of the marketing mix have now been discussed, namely: Product, Price, Place and Promotion. These four P's of the marketing mix require detailed analysis for any form of marketing to be effective. Despite the importance of the four P's several other P's should also be considered when formulating a marketing strategy. These will include:

- People (or personnel).
- Physical environment.
- Psychological variables.
- Political and economic environment.
- Programme planning.
- Process.
- Phase.
- Physical distribution.
- Profits.
- Progression and evaluation.
- Promptness and punctuality.
- Politeness.

Each of the above points will now be discussed briefly.

◆ Personnel ◆

All parts of the marketing mix are operated and managed by people.

Therefore, staffing aspects of a business are important considerations to leisure marketers.

For example, how many employees are necessary? What qualifications and experience should they possess? What duties should they perform and what salary should they receive?

The first obstacle in any business is to employ suitable staff, when recruiting new people you should:

- Develop a job description and recruitment procedure.
- Outline clearly the conditions of service and range of duties required.
- Indicate salary level.
- Indicate qualifications required, for example relevant experience, degree, driving licence.
- Indicate any advantages or benefits being offered, for example, a company car or private pension scheme.
- Provide an application form that is well structured and asks for all relevant details such as personal data, education, work experience and job-related information.
- Indicate interview date and procedure.
- Check references.
- Have an induction or on-the-job training scheme.

The people involved in each aspect of the marketing mix must be carefully co-ordinated. Although each aspect of the mix may be discussed and analysed separately, they invariably affect each other. Marketing is a people-orientated occupation and the correct choice of employee is vital. The outcome of any transaction or business activity is dependent upon the quality of personal communication. The purpose of good client liaison is not only to secure a sale but to earn respect and on-going business on a long term basis. Effective management and the profitable operation of any business depends on its staff. They are the life-blood of the business. Loyal, pleasant and productive staff are a company's greatest asset. Leisure Managers should be aware that the success of any marketing strategy is determined largely by the effectiveness of all employees from those who plan to those who implement the appropriate marketing activities.

◆ PHYSICAL ENVIRONMENT ◆

This refers to the standard of buildings or premises, decorations and furnishings of one's business or place of work. Physical environment is an extremely important aspect of marketing because the image presented to clients and customers is vital for successful business. It is well worth spending money to create a pleasant, clean and professional environment at all times.

◆ THE POLITICAL AND ECONOMIC ENVIRONMENT ◆

The political and economic environment nationally and/or internationally, often has an important impact on marketing and the productivity of any business enterprise. The level of gross national productivity, rate of inflation or level of unemployment alone are not sufficient as guides to the marketing strategies of a particular business. It is therefore necessary to look at the aggregate impact of all economic variables upon specific market segments rather than use the national economy as a sole indicator. For example, high interest rates may mean comfortable profits for specific financial enterprises, whilst they may have the opposite effect in a construction enterprise.

The object of economic environmental monitoring is to appraise the overall business status and to interpret the significance of economic change upon specific products and services that business operates. Legal constraints are usually politically influenced. They are to safeguard the public, eliminate unscrupulous dealings and to make competition as fair as possible. This aspect of the political environment is a highly specialized discipline. Professionally trained people are often used by companies to ensure that they operate within the law.

◆ PHASE ◆

This aspect of the marketing mix refers to the timing of marketing events or activities. It does not merely relate to opening hours of business but also planning marketing strategies in advance. For example, many leisure pursuits are seasonal in nature, therefore, to secure a major segment of the market advertising campaigns will have to be developed in good time so that they can be implemented at the 'correct' phase. Such campaigns have become noticeable especially during the weeks leading to Christmas, Easter and other major public holidays.

Phase, or timing, is an essential ingredient of the marketing mix. Too soon or too late in implementation will have an undesirable and cost-wasting effect.

◆ PROGRAMME PLANNING ◆

Planning a marketing programme or strategy is absolutely crucial for effective marketing and a systematic series of steps or processes need to be devised. It is clear that marketing involves many diverse principles that have to be developed within specified time constraints. Marketing is a complicated project which can easily lead to confusion when attempting to keep all its components in hand during its development and implementation. Therefore, the speeding up of one or several steps does not necessarily reduce the overall time but merely causes queues or delays whilst waiting for something else to be completed. Hence, careful and logical planning needs to be undertaken.

◆ Profits ◆

Profit making in the leisure industry has generally been confined to the private sector. However, in recent years this has become an important consideration for other leisure providers such as local authorities. The advent of competitive tendering and privatization has made businesses more competitive and accountable for their financial dealings, thus making them more cost effective.

Most leisure industries are beginning to capitalize on their various assets and distinctive qualities so that they achieve a lasting competitive superiority. They must utilize all their resources such as research, personnel development, engineering skills, production efficiency, marketing strategy and other managerial functions to the greatest economic effect. Therefore, the operation of any leisure business should be considered as a whole rather than the functioning of any one of its parts. It requires effective integration and combination of all the parts of the enterprise if effective profits are to be achieved.

The degree of profit a company makes will depend on many variables such as quality and expertise of staff, motivation of staff, technological equipment used for business operations, cost and efficiency of overheads, pricing of products and/or services, communication skills and the implementation of a marketing strategy.

◆ Physical distribution ◆

This term generally refers to the efficient movement of completed products, usually manufactured, to the consumer. The type of activities included in physical distribution might be transportation, warehousing, handling of materials, packaging, customer services and market forecasting. There are many varied types of these activities and the marketer has to decide which is the most convenient and efficient method.

Marketing, in terms of physical distribution, is an attempt to make sure that products and services are readily available to the consumer. Primarily, it is concerned with getting the right goods and providing the right service to the consumer in the right place at the right time. People depend on the goods being in a suitable and convenient place to buy or to use.

Physical distribution is concerned with the actual movement of goods from points of production to points of consumption. The product must move to the market in the most economical way that will satisfy customer service requirements. The product itself is an important factor in the selection of methods available for physical distribution. The perishability, fragility, weight and bulk are all pertinent considerations.

The objective of physical distribution is to integrate transportation, warehousing, handling, packaging and so forth into a balanced, economical effort. This aspect of the business is an important managerial consideration because a sizeable part of marketing costs is involved in this function. Thus, the marketing manager must always ask 'How efficient and effective is the physical distribution of products?'

◆ Psychological Variables ◆

Psychology plays a leading part in today's society and is used effectively in many instances as a means of influencing people's behaviour and consumption patterns. Slogans used in advertising are attempts to encourage people to buy, use, or think seriously about products or services in the ultimate hope of their being purchased. Major headlines, high-powered sales people and exploitation of the media are all methods of putting across certain issues to influence people's minds.

Such influences occasionally go unnoticed by customers in that the techniques used to sell items are so discreet. An almost everyday example exists in supermarkets. Why is it that counters are frequently altered in their product content? A regular customer may go to get a specific product and discover it has been shelved elsewhere. Whilst looking for this product, another product may catch the customer's attention. The customer may be tempted to purchase this particular item. Similarly, more common items such as sugar, tea and coffee are usually placed high or low on the shelves and new or older products placed at eye level, thus they may catch people's attention and tempt them to a purchase. Finally, at every checkout point there is a selection of confectionery items, magazines and other small products which a customer might place in their trolley whilst waiting. As a result of these psychological techniques, nearly every shopper buys more than they originally intended.

Psychological variables can also be used to advantage to increase participation levels in sports centres. Therefore, effective Leisure Managers need to consider the effects of various psychological variables when planning a marketing strategy.

◆ Promptness and punctuality ◆

These are a definite requirement for providing an effective service, especially in developing a long-term relationship with customers. It goes without saying that goods must be delivered promptly and punctually in order to develop and maintain goodwill. Such qualities will have a knock-on effect: satisfied customers will spread goodwill through word of mouth, thus capturing a greater segment of the market.

Customers rapidly become dissatisfied when these qualities are absent or poorly applied. The important point to remember is: 'goods do not come back, but customers do'. The same principles apply to services.

◆ Politeness ◆

Marketing does not only involve theoretical knowledge, but also communications with a variety of people. Politeness is important to create and maintain good relations with customers and colleagues alike.

One may have to readily accept mistakes, rectify them as soon as possible and continue to operate smoothly. The adage that 'the customer is always right' may have to be accepted, although reluctantly in some cases. The customer must be kept happy and satisfied. Goodwill and quality of service must always prevail. Politeness after all does not cost anything but it can gain rewards.

◆ Progression and evaluation ◆

Since leisure marketing is a rather expensive and very time consuming exercise, it is important that some method of measuring progression and of evaluation be adopted. The monitoring of progression and evaluation is an important aspect of all managerial functions, including marketing.

Progression may simply be the extent of improvement or level a given function has developed or reached. Both are important considerations when one considers the extent of marketing and its many ramifications (e.g. the P's included in the marketing mix).

Evaluation may be regarded as the process by which the value of something is judged. The process of evaluation begins with the formulation of certain objectives, moves on to how they are to be attained and finishes with analysis and appraisal of results.

A critical review of all marketing procedures, in relation to marketing objectives, must be made if the desired results are to be attained. This will require a continuous process of reviewing the objectives, procedures and goals, in relation to each other. The ultimate purpose of monitoring progression and evaluation is to provide feedback and ensure that the marketing strategy is effectively and efficiently executed.

◆ Conclusion ◆

Having described briefly a variety of components which can be regarded as the marketing mix, it should have become evident that leisure marketing is a complex discipline to put into practice effectively. Most major texts on marketing will describe the marketing mix as the four P's, namely, Product, Place, Price and Promotion. However, several other P's can be regarded as pertinent to marketing and require serious consideration.

Although the marketing mix has been described as a series of separate entities, it must be remembered that all the components described, that is all the P's, must be viewed as a whole so that they become integrated into an effective, functional operation. In order for this to take place, one further consideration requires explanation, that of market research.

◆ Discussion questions ◆

1. What role do you think marketing plays in effective leisure management? Give reasons for your comments.

2. Discuss and describe the values of the different sources available to market a specific leisure facility or service.

3. Explain the role of the A.I.D.A. principle to leisure marketing.

4. Evaluate some of the P's relating to marketing and describe how these may prove effective to leisure management.

5. Highlight, with brief comments, the various ways a Leisure Manager may promote a specific facility, programme or service of your choice.

◆ Case study ◆

Mrs. Anne Johnson was a newly appointed Manageress of the Keenan Venture Park. Her main task was to market the facility and to attract more customers. Since marketing was one of her strengths, she decided to design a marketing and advertising campaign. With the help of her staff, she developed an advertising strategy. Mrs. Johnson decided to place a series of advertisements in local newspapers and four national magazines related to park themes. This she felt would help to keep the venture park in the public eye over several months. Arrangements and contracts were signed by Mrs. Johnson and the various advertising agencies she was to use. However, after only six weeks, she received from her Directors, a letter stating that all spending must cease forthwith, due to the financial difficulties the company was facing. This posed a dilemma for Mrs. Johnson.

1. What implications now confront Mrs. Johnson?

2. How effective do you think the advertising campaign would have been, taking into account the careful planning, design and thought gone into it?

3. What rationale or actions should the Directors make, or should they stand by their initial stance of ceasing all spending?

Leisure Marketing: Research, Segmentation and Targeting

*M*arket research plays a vital role for Leisure Managers and is a necessary requirement if their managerial skills are to be most effective. It basically involves the gathering of information or data which may be 'qualitative' or 'quantitative' in nature. The distinction is made by Crouch (1984) as follows:

> 'Qualitative research is so called because its emphasis lies in producing data which is rich in insight, understanding, explanation and depth of information, but which cannot be justified statistically . . . is typically carried out with only a few respondents.' [24]

Examples are in-depth interviews and group discussions, where the time-scale involved is small, and information gathered more quickly and less expensively than in quantitative research.

*Q*uantitative research according to Crouch 'involves the research techniques of representative samples, questionnaires, interviews, data processing and so on'. Such in-depth analysis enables the researcher to make concluding statements such as: 55% of the population under-use their leisure time, or 72% of members use the swimming pool. Hence, quantitative research is more time consuming, both in terms of gathering and analysing the data.

*M*arket research is an objective method designed by a company to collect data concerning such issues as:

- Customer response to a new product.
- Consumer purchase behaviour for purposes of targeting a specific market.
- Maximising sales.
- Finding out what services prospective customers want.
- Evaluating the effect and impact of various marketing strategies.
- Utilizing resources more fully.
- Tapping possible marketing opportunities.
- Fostering quality control of goods and services.
- Discovering how to make resources more cost effective.

Market research has these and many other applications, although it requires special skills to put into practice and to interpret and analyse any data that may have been collected.

Market research requires a methodical approach, although the exact procedure will depend on precisely what is to be researched, the following guidelines might prove useful for Leisure Managers:

- Formulate the problem — often poses problems to managers in that they do not know exactly what problem they want to research. A clear statement, however, needs to be made before any corrective action can take place.

- Gather preliminary information — involves speaking to people within the company about the problem to be researched and in some cases, also speaking to external advisors. The gathering of such information is only exploratory but will help in the preliminary research.

- Plan and conduct a formal investigation — certainly the most time-consuming stage of market research, this requires specific research techniques, designs and procedures, some of which we shall now discuss. Essentially there are three major methods of gathering information for research purposes, the survey method, the observational method and the experimental method.

◆ THE SURVEY METHOD ◆

This involves gathering information by asking a random sample of people a series of questions. This well-tried method is useful when trying to discover the opinions of customers. However, surveys are time-consuming and it is difficult to acquire accurate and meaningful data from respondents.

A survey may be conducted either by mail, telephone or in person. Each approach has its own advantages and disadvantages. The first approach generally involves the use of a questionnaire, and since this is still a common method used in leisure market research, it will be discussed separately and in more detail on p. 72. For the moment, it is sufficient to say that forms suitable for gathering data should allow relevant information to be recorded in a clear and logical manner so that when the data collection is completed, information can readily be used for statistical or analytical purposes. The form may have several rows, columns and headings, the number depending on the nature, extent and type of data to be recorded.

A telephone survey can seek responses to questions requiring short answers and the information is obtained rather quickly. It is a flexible method but costs would rise if the survey included a large geographical area. A major disadvantage is that people can refuse to participate simply by hanging up the telephone.

The personal interview can become expensive and time-consuming, but is the most flexible of the three methods. Questions can be re-phrased or explained more fully and a favourable relationship can be developed between the interviewer and respondent. However, the former must avoid allowing personal bias into the interview situation.

◆ THE OBSERVATION METHOD ◆

This is rather a basic method which involves watching and recording events as they occur. Devices such as video cameras and recorders can be used. Examples of the observation survey method being used are: establishing how long customers have to wait to get service; time spans at queues or check-out points and whether shoppers congregate in specific areas.

This method has the advantage of being relatively inexpensive, and direct contact with the public is avoided if need be. However, observations are subject to bias and clear indications cannot be derived as to why respondents act as they do.

◆ THE EXPERIMENTAL METHOD ◆

This is used to gather information in an attempt to establish a cause-and-effect relationship by controlling one variable and trying to produce a desired effect in another variable. This method is used frequently and especially with the testing of new products.

The advantage of this form of research is that actual cause-and-effect relationships can be identified in a scientific manner to aid the leisure marketer in future decisions. A major drawback in conducting controlled experiments, however, is the difficulty of controlling the variables.

◆ ANALYSIS OF DATA ◆

Whatever method has been used, once all the data has been gathered, it must be categorized, tabulated and summarized so that processing and interpretation of results can take place.

In all major forms of research, data should be analysed statistically if any level of reliability is to be assumed, or recommendations made. Statistics is a very specialized subject and too diverse to discuss in detail. However, there are numerous texts on statistics and everyone involved in any form of research should make themselves conversant with the various tests available. The discussion and interpretation of analysed data should explain the various findings which support or reject the original hypothesis. Often the presentation of data will include various tables, charts and/or diagrams so that the analysed data can be more readily and easily understood by the reader. Eventually, the researcher should be able to make certain conclusions and recommendations and represent the actual outcomes and benefits, if any, of the entire research.

◆ QUESTIONNAIRES ◆

Questionnaires have been used for gathering data and information for many decades and are still widely used in all forms of research. This method is still extensively used by Leisure Managers. Following our brief comments on p. 70, we now discuss them in greater depth.

In developing a questionnaire many important principles need to be considered. Firstly, a thorough understanding of the particular field being researched and the nature of the data required needs to be attained. It must be remembered that a questionnaire involves a series of questions which is mailed or given to selected participants for completion. If a questionnaire is mailed it is free from any bias since it is often returned anonymously.

A questionnaire is a form designed to secure responses to certain questions. Generally, such questions are factual, that is, intended to obtain information about a service or a product of which a respondent is assumed to have knowledge. Questions can be singled out about particular aspects regarded as significant to the purpose of the research.

Crouch indicates that a questionnaire serves four main purposes:

- ◆ To collect relevant data.
- ◆ To make data comparable.
- ◆ To minimize bias.
- ◆ To motivate respondents.

The questionnaire can also be used as a major instrument for gathering data from a varied and widely scattered source. It is particularly useful when personal contact is hindered, by, for example, distance or considered unnecessary.

Essentially, a questionnaire should be developed in such a way that the respondent feels obliged or motivated to complete it. This aspect is important although often overlooked. It is reasonable to assume that questionnaires go to people who are very busy and short of time. They must be devised so as to take up the minimum of the respondent's time. The adage, KISS, Keep It Short and Simple, is one worth remembering.

The market researcher should try and ensure respondents give honest and accurate answers. An additional aim would be to secure the sympathy and co-operation of the respondent. These considerations are important, for in many cases, recipients of a questionnaire are not personally interested in the researcher or the investigation itself.

Questions may be of two types. Questions may be 'closed', that is, a list of answers is supplied and the respondent has to choose one answer. In closed questions it is essential to allow for all possible answers so that the categories provided are both exhaustive and mutually exclusive. Closed questions are commonly used to secure categorized data. They are time-saving for the respondent and quick to analyse. However, such questions may force respondents to choose a category which does not reflect their true status.

The other type of question technique is 'open-ended'. This provides or offers a respondent the opportunity to express more about the question in detail. An example would be, 'what advantages do you envisage when the local sports centre opens?' Such a question will, in many cases, get information on what respondents really think. However, open-ended questions present difficulties of analysis and tabulation.

It is often wise to include both types of question in a questionnaire to make it more interesting and allow for a better layout of the form. It is important to allow sufficient space for response on the form following open-ended questions.

A questionnaire is more likely to be used by a respondent if certain points are taken into consideration, such as: Are some questions really necessary? Are the responses simple? Do they avoid specific detail? Is the question clear with definitive limitations? These and many other questions must be considered when constructing and formulating a questionnaire.

The problem with any questionnaire is in determining its validity. It is unlikely that any questionnaire will be totally valid. However, Good and Scates (1954) developed an eight item validity check for questionnaires. They are still relevant and important features to consider in the development of questionnaire. A summary of their validity check is itemized below:

- Is the question on the subject? Does it effectively exclude irrelevant factors — those not desired? Does the question contribute something that is unique, that it is not duplicated?

- Is the question perfectly clear and unambiguous? Are its implications clearly understood?
- Does the question get at something stable, something relatively deep-seated, well considered, non-superficial, and not ephemeral, but something which is typical of the individual or of the situation?
- Will the question be responded to by a large enough proportion of people to permit it to have validity? Does it seem to be engaging enough to get responses with some depth and reality?
- Do the responses show a reasonable range of variation? (This only applies if variation is expected).
- Is the information obtained consistent? Does it agree with predictions? Does it fit in with the general pattern of information which is obtained?
- Is the full scope and intent of the question so clearly indicated that the respondent will not omit parts of the responses through lack of certainty as to what the question desires?
- Is there a possibility of using an external criteria to evaluate the questionnaire? [25]

Having devised the questions for your questionnaire, it now needs to be pre-tested to weed out any flaws before the final draft is completed. Pre-testing may have to be done on more than one occasion.

The essence of developing a questionnaire is to keep it short and simple (KISS) and to avoid ambiguity. In spite of careful considerations, there is no such thing as an ideal questionnaire. However, it must be developed attractively so that recipients feel the need or incentive to respond with honest and accurate information. Furthermore, one must ensure, as far as possible that the recipient has the relevant information at his or her disposal and that he or she is free and willing to respond.

◆ Advantages of questionnaires ◆

It is worth highlighting some of the major advantages of questionnaires, since this type of research technique will continue to be used. The advantages must be weighed against the disadvantages:

- They permit a wide geographic coverage with a minimum outlay of expense and effort.
- They can reach people who are difficult to contact.
- Greater coverage makes for greater validity in the results by promoting

the selection of a larger and more representative sample of respondents.

- If a questionnaire does not ask for a signature or other means of identification, it may elicit more objective information because of its impersonality.
- More detailed and elaborate information is given by respondents who are allowed to seek or check reliable information prior to answering.
- Questionnaires allow for greater uniformity in the manner in which the questions are posed. This ensures greater comparability in the answers. However, it does not necessarily ensure true and honest replies.

◆ Disadvantages of questionnaires ◆

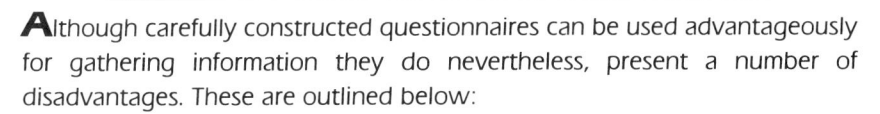

Although carefully constructed questionnaires can be used advantageously for gathering information they do nevertheless, present a number of disadvantages. These are outlined below:

- Questionnaires do not permit the researcher to note the apparent reluctance or evasiveness of his or her respondents. Such matters are best dealt with in personal interviews.
- They do not permit the researcher to follow through on any misleading questions or inadequate answers.
- Non-returns are a major weakness of questionnaires and reduce the sample size on which the results and findings are based.
- Biased answers can result from factors such as interest in certain questions only, attitudes, educational and socio-economic status and the conscientiousness of the respondent.
- The validity of all data depends in a crucial way on the ability and willingness of respondents to provide the necessary information required. Sometimes respondents, though capable of providing the information, may not be willing to part with such information. This is more likely in questions concerning sensitive issues or that reflect personally on the respondent.
- Questionnaires rarely provide the researcher with sufficient opportunity to develop the rapport necessary for asking questions of a personal nature.
- The researcher is unaware of the inability or unwillingness of respondents to providing the requested information, consequently, they are unable to judge the extent of the invalidity of their data.
- A major problem with any questionnaire is the possibility of

misinterpretation of questions. This danger obviously increases if questions are ambiguous.

It is worth noting that many of the disadvantages above can be alleviated if attention is paid to the presentation of the questions.

◆ MARKET SEGMENTATION ◆

The isolation of specific markets is referred to as market segmentation. It is the process of dividing the total market into smaller parts made up of customers with similar characteristics and interests, such as, similar behavioural patterns, lifestyles or goals. Marketing objectives can only be achieved through action in selected and specific markets, regardless of the diversity of leisure company activities, so the process of segmentation is vital to planning a marketing strategy and the various market segments offer a schedule or scheme for the concentration of marketing resources. No two companies will view segmentation in the same way. How a company targets its advertising will thus serve as a means of identifying competitor's activities.

If any segmentation of a market is to be useful in strategic planning, it must consider certain characteristics:

- ◆ The market segment must have adequate revenue to justify its inclusion within the marketing strategy.
- ◆ The market segment must have adequate stability to allow sufficient time to achieve both financial, functional or operating objectives.
- ◆ The market segment should if possible be measurable to ensure effective evaluation of marketing efforts.
- ◆ The selected segment must be accessible to justify its operating costs.
- ◆ The market segment must be sizeable to ensure enough potential customers to generate a degree of profit.
- ◆ The selected market segment must contain a degree of responsiveness in that people in the segment are willing to buy the product or service.

Having considered the various criteria for market segmentation, it is often difficult to identify or establish market segments effectively. However, this difficulty can be alleviated if the manager considers four broad dimensions: demographical, geographical, psychological and behavioural.

◆ DEMOGRAPHICAL SEGMENTATION ◆

This divides people into groups according to age, gender, families, households, occupation, income and education, to name those most commonly used.

This method of segmentation is used when the market is divided into groups that are relatively easy to quantify and find. They represent important indicators for the different elements of a market and can be useful for effective marketing.

Demographical trends are often studied by marketers to enable them to predict changes in their markets. Population numbers and trends will help determine the demands for leisure products and services in the future. Taking age as an example, leisure marketers are interested in the number of people in various age groups with a view to relevant provision of services and products. The present trend appears to be for fewer young people, due to the falling birth rate, and more elderly people, due to medical advances.

The other demographical variables of gender, families, households, occupation, income and educational attainment will all play a significant and important role in determining specific market segments.

◆ GEOGRAPHICAL SEGMENTATION ◆

Geographical segmentation divides people into groups according to where they live. Geophysical characteristics of where people live are perhaps the most commonly used segmental divisions since where people live strongly affects their needs, wants and interests. Geographical segments can vary in size; the division may be into villages, towns, cities, counties, regions or even nations. The division may not depend solely on location; but on geophysical considerations such as climate. For example, depending on the product or service being offered a region may be targeted for its predominance of snow or sunshine throughout the year.

◆ PSYCHOLOGICAL SEGMENTATION ◆

Psychological segmentation relates to variations in people's attitudes, and beliefs, which in turn determine their decisions to purchase an item or participate in a given activity. Psychological segmentation plays an increasingly vital role in leisure marketing. Variables such as lifestyle, interests, activities, personality and self-image have an important impact on leisure.

Psychological characteristics vary depending on such factors as age and gender (demographical considerations) and location (geographical considerations). Manufacturers and marketing managers can often exploit psychological factors, such as the desire to be accepted in a group. Manufacturers of running shoes, for example, have been particularly successful in the use of this factor in advertising their product.

Personality traits have for a long time been used, relatively successfully, by marketers. People exhibiting certain traits tend to share common preferences. For example, the typical extrovert may prefer sports cars to hatchbacks for their aggressive image and appeal. By contrast, the typical introvert may prefer a hatchback as this will attract less attention.

People's self-image is also an important psychological variable that is often reflected in buying behaviour. Marketers are constantly trying to match a product closely with the consumer's persona. People's possessions and activities project their personalities and maintain or improve their image. The marketing of fashion clothing is a clear example of the exploitation of how consumers see or would like to project themselves.

◆ BEHAVIOURAL SEGMENTATION ◆

People's behaviour can be considered in terms of individual or group behaviour. The need to analyse how and why consumers behave as they do, is vital for the leisure marketer. Those who understand consumer behaviour, are more likely to make better marketing decisions. We shall now discuss some aspects of behavioural segmentation in detail.

◆ ATTITUDE ◆

Attitude may be regarded as the form of response given to an idea or object. These responses may be favourable or unfavourable. Attitudes help people to adjust to different situations and provide direction to consumer behaviour.

◆ MOTIVES ◆

Motives may be regarded as inner forces that control a person's behaviour. Most motives come from psychological and social situations. Leisure marketers must strive to show how their products and services can support the motives of consumers.

◆ PERCEPTION ◆

Perception generally refers to the process in which incoming stimuli are organized and interpreted. People are constantly bombarded by a myriad of stimuli. Perception is therefore selective, because people cannot focus or contend with all the stimuli surrounding them at once. A successful leisure marketer will use stimuli that hold a customer's attention and produce an accurate perception of what is being promoted. This is particularly apparent in advertising. People's perceptions can be affected by needs, wants, motives, interests, attitudes, opinions, values, past experience and memory.

◆ LEARNING ABILITIES ◆

Learning abilities vary enormously among individuals. Learning can be regarded as a relatively permanent change in behaviour or thinking. Leisure marketers should attempt to acquire some knowledge of how consumers learn because marketing strategies can have a major influence in helping them remember names, products or brands, prices, locations, services, logos and perhaps special promotions.

◆ Group behaviour ◆

The above very briefly discusses factors in individual human behaviour, but behavioural patterns can also be influenced by group associations. Consumers are social people; they interact with other people, share common values, and join organizations or clubs. We shall now look at some group influences on behaviour.

◆ Cultural values ◆

Cultural values exist when a set of learned values, attitudes and behavioural expectations are shared by all within a particular cultural group. Cultural values can be learned through various sources including family, school, church, sports teams, youth clubs and a host of voluntary organizations.

◆ Social status ◆

Social status relates to the various groups of people with similar lifestyles, values, behaviour and interests. If a large enough number of consumers have similar characteristics, it is a potential market segment and target market. Whenever leisure products or services are appropriate to a given group, leisure markets should respond with marketing techniques that are appealing and attractive.

◆ Reference groups ◆

Reference groups consist of a number of people who share similar values and interests, meet and interact regularly and, in general, influence each other, for example, a drama society. Reference groups of all sizes can serve as excellent sources for target markets.

◆ Family interactions ◆

Family interactions are a very common target for marketers. Families will tend to share common values and goals and communicate relatively freely. Many choose major consumer goods on the basis of collective agreement, for example, cars, food, clothing, holidays, home furnishings and insurance.

Finally, the scope of market segmentation for leisure purposes is summarized in Table I.

Demographical	Geographical	Psychological	Behavioural
Population	Villages	Lifestyle	*INDIVIDUAL*
Age	Towns	Interests	Attitudes
Gender	Cities	Activities	Motives
Family size	Counties	Personality traits	Perceptions
Household	Regions	Self-Image	Learning abilities
Occupation	Nations	Opinions	*GROUP*
Income			Cultural values
Education			Social status
			Reference groups
			Family-interactions

Table 1 The scope of leisure market segmentation

♦ TARGET MARKETING ♦

Most leisure agencies or businesses have to operate against competition in large markets and with limited resources. Many are unable to 'sell' with equal efficiency and success to the entire market or every market segment. Therefore, it becomes necessary for reasons of efficiency and economics, to select target markets.

Target marketing is a technique in which a marketer, having identified the different customer segments relevant to his or her products and services, selects one or more as a specific target. Marketers then try to gain benefits from satisfying selected segments as opposed to attempting to satisfy the entire market.

Leisure marketers have three policy options available to them when considering their target marketing strategies: undifferentiated, differentiated and concentrated marketing.

♦ UNDIFFERENTIATED MARKETING ♦

Leisure marketers who adopt this policy produce a single product and hope to get as many customers as possible to buy it. They do not market to different segments, that is, they ignore market segmentation entirely. The undifferentiated method involves the use of one product and one marketing approach that will appeal to the largest number of potential customers in the market.

An undifferentiated marketing strategy appears to work best when product items have relatively few features, such as, paper towels or tissues and polystyrene cups. In such cases, customers perceive very little difference between competitive brands other than perhaps in their packaging and advertising. However, a major disadvantage of this technique is that if customer needs are not met satisfactorily, competitors will arrive in the market to reduce the gap between what customers want and what they are getting.

◆ Differentiated Marketing ◆

This type of marketing technique is used when a leisure company introduces different versions of the same products, programmes or services each aimed at a different group of potential customers. Leisure marketers employ this technique where they identify several different segments in the market relevant to their products and services.

◆ Concentrated Marketing ◆

This strategy aims at one market segment only in an attempt to market the best possible product or service. In other words, a company attempts to produce the ideal or 'perfect' product for a single segment of the market, for example, Rolls Royce cars. The object of concentrated marketing is to obtain a strong market share in a very specific segment. This may involve status, high price, power or economy.

A major advantage of concentrated marketing is the outstanding reputation a company may achieve as a specialist serving a certain market segment. However, the business may be at risk in relying on a single segment of a single market if that single market collapses for some reason.

◆ Conclusion ◆

Leisure marketing is far from being a dull subject and should prove to be a very challenging task for Leisure Managers. Successful leisure management will rest very heavily on the implementation of marketing strategies and the effort given to them.

All businesses rely heavily on marketing to sell products and services to people. Leisure marketing is a complex affair, encompassing many varied business activities. Such activities include market research, planning of products and services, transportation, storing, advertising, financing, market segmentation and communication skills. These only represent a few activities that need consideration when contemplating leisure marketing.

Leisure Managers must ask themselves six basic marketing questions when formulating a marketing strategy:

1. Who are the target customers I want to reach?

2. Where do they live and work?

3. What do they want from my product and/or service?

4. What marketing strategy do I need to develop to reach my target customers?

5. How much will this cost me?

6. What price are customers prepared to pay?

For a leisure marketer to achieve any degree of success, a study of the various marketing concepts should be made. The time and effort devoted to marketing in terms of acquiring knowledge will play a vital role in determining the degree of any manager's success.

DISCUSSION QUESTIONS

1. Describe the benefits that a Leisure Manager may derive from conducting market research.

2. Discuss some of the factors involved in leisure market research.

3. Choose a particular leisure environment or facility you wish to develop, and discuss how you would conduct your market research to ascertain whether there is a market for your project.

4. What are the advantages of using questionnaires to seek information?

5. What precautions do you need to take when formulating a questionnaire?

◆ Case study ◆

Mr. G. Anderson, the centre manager, realizes that the new hydropool adjacent to the swimming pool is not being used to any great extent. Before venturing on an advertising campaign, he decides to seek possible reasons for the apparent lack of use or interest.

Since Mr. Anderson was going to be busy for the next few weeks, he asked his two junior assistants, to devise a questionnaire to give to existing users of the centre. The questionnaire was soon developed and distributed to customers, who were asked to return it on their next visit to the centre.

Over 500 copies of the questionnaire were produced and over a two week period approximately 450 were distributed. A further two weeks had elapsed, which was the deadline for return of the questionnaire, and only 220 had been returned.

On analysing the returned questionnaires, many had been incorrectly completed. In effect, only about 105 questionnaires were of any value. Mr. Anderson soon began to realize the whole exercise was a failure.

1. Why did Mr. Anderson regard the questionnaire exercise to be a failure?

2. What procedures and precautions should have been taken to prevent such a failure?

3. Who is to blame for the questionnaire failure and why?

Leisure Management

The diverse nature of leisure activities means that the Leisure Manager is confronted with a complexity of managerial and practical administrative tasks ranging from the provision and utilization of facilities and services, to dealing with customers, from staffing to marketing and from financial planning to maintenance. The list is by no means exhaustive.

Two major arguments exist among management theorists. The first claims that if a person is a successful manager, then he or she can manage anything equally as well, thus suggesting that management principles are the same in any area. The second refutes this claim arguing that knowledge, skills and experience of one's trade are essential to successful management. For example, a successful manufacturer cannot automatically become a successful Leisure Manager.

Management principles may be the same regardless of the nature of business, but they have to be modified and adapted to suit the particular situation in question, and take into account the knowledge, skills and experience of the manager. Many of today's management principles stem from early theories.

This chapter outlines some of these management theories because they may influence today's Leisure Managers. They will serve as guidelines only, for they will have to be modified before being implemented. It is impossible to construct rigid principles, since no two leisure agencies are the same. The success of a Leisure Manager depends on the manager him or herself, the staff, size of budget, and the local political climate amongst other criteria. A successful Leisure Manager in one leisure complex will not automatically be successful in another.

Successful leisure management entails the application of diverse administrative and management concepts to control the processes that mobilize a company's resources, both human and material, and to attain its predetermined aims.

The terms 'administration' and 'management' are frequently used and interchanged. The latter is usually regarded as the overall concept, whereas *administration* is a part of management. Brech (1963) makes the distinction as follows:

> *Administration* — 'That part of the management process concerned with the institution and carrying out of procedures by which the programme is laid down and communicated, and the progress of activities is regulated and checked against targets and plans.'
>
> *Management* — 'A social process entailing responsibility for the effective and economical planning and regulation of the operations of an enterprise, in fulfilment of a given purpose or task.' [26]

It is clear from the above descriptions that management encompasses a variety of administrative functions, so we will use the term 'management' even though some administrative functions will be described. Management for our purpose can be regarded as the guidance, leadership and control of the efforts of individuals pursuing common goals in the most efficient manner.

◆ THE MANAGEMENT PROCESS ◆

Every leisure organization or company requires personnel with management skills so that its operations can be conducted smoothly and efficiently. Many basic processes or techniques are common to the majority of management endeavours. The identification of the various management skills will provide sound guidelines for the successful achievement of one's aims.

One approach to exploring the various processes involved in leisure management is to analyse the problems that may confront Leisure Managers and to relate them to the process of problem-solving. Processes involved in leisure management are briefly summarized below:

- ◆ Planning — All management procedures should be concerned with the process of planning or deciding what has to be done. Leisure products, services or programmes all require meticulous planning if management is to be effective and efficient.

- ◆ Directing — Leisure Managers are confronted with numerous tasks and will frequently have to direct, delegate or issue orders and instructions so that various management procedures are fulfilled.

- ◆ Resourcing — Another major concern for Leisure Managers is the ability to utilize resources to the full or to know when additional resources are required for effective management. More discerning managers will be able to detect wasteful, inefficient or uneconomical use of resources perhaps due to outdated equipment or time-consuming procedures.

- ◆ Organizing — The ability to organize is an essential skill for every Leisure Manager. It is often felt that there are never enough hours in the day to accomplish all intended tasks. Organizing requires planning, the allocation of work or tasks and the formulation of a structural framework within a leisure company, or organization, so that various tasks can be identified within it.

- Time management — The management of time is an issue which is fundamental to job performance and is an essential requirement for the Leisure Manager. Time management involves utilizing time effectively and setting priorities. Leisure Managers must make time to plan; time spent on planning will save time in the long term.

- Staffing — Leisure Managers are responsible for their staff and it is important for them to seek staff who have the expertise and experience to utilize resources and accomplish the aims of the company.

- Controlling — It is essential that Leisure Managers know what goes on within the company and maintain control of all tasks and operations being conducted. They must know whether staff are conforming to agreed plans and meeting the standards set by the company.

- Co-ordination of staff and tasks — This plays a vital role in successful leisure management, for it helps the smooth functioning of team effort and reduces any unnecessary duplication of work. It is a particularly important skill in a large expanding company with an increasing number of products and services on offer.

- Evaluation — This is an on-going process of constant reappraisal. It enables objectives to be accomplished and the maintenance or improvement of existing services. These concerns are applicable to Leisure Managers in the light of today's competitive environment.

The summary above offers only a brief account of some major aspects of the management processes which are encountered by today's Leisure Managers. Many of these aspects have their foundations in theories put forward by various authors during the early part of this century. The number and depth of these theories is too extensive to review in this text. However, several major principles are briefly discussed below.

◆ HENRY FAYOL (1841–1925) ◆

As early as 1916, Fayol, a French industrialist, outlined his principles of management. These were not translated into English until 1949, hence his contributions were not widely known and implemented until comparatively recently and during the intervening years, other authors were to make additional contributions to management theory. Fayol was aware that the problems of personnel and management were the key to industrial unrest and he attempted to apply a scientific method as a solution. In his approach, he examined three aspects of management:

- The 'Activities' of an organization.
- The 'Elements' of management.
- The 'Principles' of management.

◆ THE ACTIVITIES OF AN ◆ ORGANIZATION — WHAT THE ORGANIZATION DOES

Fayol was of the opinion that all activities within an industrial organization are contained in six categories, namely:

- Technical activities (production and manufacturing).
- Commercial activities (buying, selling and marketing).
- Financial activities (budgeting and making best use of capital).
- Managerial activities (organizing and planning).
- Security services (the protection of people and property).
- Accounting services (book-keeping, statistics and stock-taking).

These six categories were regarded as present in any organization regardless of its size or complexity, although with varying degrees of prominence.

◆ THE 'ELEMENTS' OF ◆ MANAGEMENT — WHAT MANAGEMENT DOES

Fayol was concerned with the process of management: the actual job of a manager. This led him to identify five elements of management which he regarded as being universal to all managers of all organizations, to manage is to forecast and plan, to organize, to command, to co-ordinate and to control.

- To forecast and plan – This basically refers to assessing the future, looking ahead and planning for it. This may take into account short and long-term plans.

- To organize – Fayol refers to this element as the division of material and human resources within an organization. This includes the division of labour amongst employees so that all activities lead to the better use of resources.

- To command – Fayol stressed the need for an organization to maintain an active rather than a passive state. He was conscious of the need to keep all employees active. For this element to be effective, it was necessary for managers to develop leadership skills so that his or her subordinates gave the best possible performance.

- To co-ordinate – A manager must attempt to keep his or her functions in line with the total and overall objectives of the organization. This entails regular meetings or exchange of information so that unity and bonding of the organization is achieved.
- To control – All organizations set standards and these have to be met by certain controlling techniques, such as, regular inspection or quality control and monitoring performance. In order for aims and objectives to be met, control of all activities must be exercised.

These elements postulated by Fayol are similar to those outlined earlier in *The Management Process*. However, according to Fayol, these five elements are only part of the management process, for he also outlined various principles of management that managers must take into account.

◆ THE 'PRINCIPLES' OF MANAGEMENT ◆

Fayol put forward fourteen principles of management he considered necessary, although they were not intended to be used rigidly in every situation, but rather as the situation demanded. These principles are rather diverse in nature, but it is sufficient for our purposes to give a brief account and explanation.

- Division of work – This concept basically refers to specialization: the fewer tasks a person undertakes in his or her job, the more efficient, skilled and effective they become. However, too few tasks can lead to rather unhappy and dull lives because of boredom and the repetitive nature of the job.
- Accountability and responsibility – Fayol regarded these principles as going hand-in-hand managers are ultimately accountable to their superiors and responsible for their staff.
- Discipline – This principle, together with obedience and behaviour, is of necessity at all levels for the smooth operation of a business. Fayol felt that if workers and management agree, then discipline is not too difficult. Hence, he was in favour of collective bargaining. In essence, discipline is best achieved by (a) good superiors at all levels, (b) agreements as clear and as fair as possible and (c) sanctions or penalties applied judiciously.
- Unity of command – This concept refers to the fact that each subordinate or worker has only one immediate superior or boss. If this principle becomes violated, according to Fayol, authority becomes undermined, discipline becomes jeopardized, order disturbed and the stability of the business becomes threatened.
- Unity of direction – In instances where there is a group of activities sharing the same objectives, there must be one plan to achieve the

co-ordination of the efforts headed by one person: a group of activities should have one head, one plan and one set of objectives.

- Subordination of individual interest to the general interest – This principle refers to the idea that the interests of an organization must come before any individual. Today's concept might be to attempt to make individual objectives compatible with those of the organization and vice versa. Implementing such a principle calls for firmness and good example by managers.

- Remuneration (payment) of personnel – The pay structure of any organization plays a vital role in its survival. Factors, such as bonuses, fair pay, profit-sharing and commission scales should all be considered so that the best and most appropriate scheme meets mutual agreement. In spite of such considerations, Fayol accepted the fact that there is no such thing as a perfect system.

- Centralization – This concept states that there should be one central point in the organization that exercises control over all its sections or departments. However, this might not prove practical or ideal in very large organizations or corporations, since these may prefer decentralization. This latter concept refers to control being divided into small, independently run divisions. Most organizations try to aim for a balance between the two. Centralization facilitates consultation and communication between departments. Decentralization creates more participation in decision-making processes at lower levels and local decisions can be made there and then.

- The Scalar chain – This is the 'chain of command': an organization is composed of a chain of superiors ranging from the highest ranks to the lowest. Fayol felt that this chain should be preserved, in that communications move up or down the chain passing through every link with no 'jumping of the queue'. Unfortunately, this is a very time-consuming exercise, especially in large organizations and will be of very little value when dealing with urgent cases.

- Order – Fayol firmly believed that material and social order is of managerial necessity. He advocated that there is a place for everything, and everything has its place. Similarly for people, a place for everyone and everyone in his or her place.

- Equity – Managers should show signs of kindness and justice so that subordinates remain loyal and devoted.

- Stability of personnel – A stable workforce will enhance efficiency.

- Initiative – This principle is applied when management encourages staff to work out a successful plan of action, thus taking an active part in decision-making.

- *Esprit de Corps* – At all times staff morale must be fostered so that a common sense of purpose is achieved. This principle of management is associated with the term 'motivation'. If this is stirred among all employees, a more willing and effective workforce ensues.

Fayol paved the way to management theory and many of his ideas and thoughts should prove useful to Leisure Managers, although with some modification.

◆ FREDERICK W. TAYLOR (1856–1915) ◆

Taylor was another theorist who made a major impact on management thinking. He made great efforts to produce 'the best' or 'ideal' method of management and also applied a scientific approach to his theories. He aimed to maximize efficiency in an organization so that profits could be maximized and he made the following three assumptions:

- People could be regarded as being similar to machines, and made as efficient as possible.
- Correctly applied incentives would make people work harder to increase their earnings.
- Employees would see the need to cooperate with management. The financial rewards from doing so would benefit the organization in terms of increased profits, and employees in terms of increased salaries.

Taylor, a practicing industrial manager, soon realized that many shortcomings were prevalent among managers. He regarded inefficiency, stemming from managers failing to find ways to co-ordinate and control output from the workforce and their failure to develop a fair and satisfactory method of paying employees, as a serious failure. Similarly, he considered that managers who had not analysed workers' methods of working to discover better ways of using the workforce were failing in their jobs.

Science played a major role in Taylor's thinking. He attempted to make management a science resting on fixed principles as opposed to mere vague ideas. He devised such methods as job study, work study, time study, method study, control of work flow and incentives. In today's terms, we would say that Taylor advocated the doctrine of 'cost effectiveness', this doctrine implies control, and control is the central theme of Taylor's work.

Taylor assumed that every organization and its employees wanted 'maximum prosperity'. In spite of this assumption, strikes and conflicts still occurred so he made three suggestions to account for them:

- Employees feared that increased output would create fewer jobs.

- Poor management caused employees to 'go slow' to protect themselves.
- Inefficient ways of doing jobs were prevalent.

These three problems, which are still encountered today to varying degrees, were alleviated to some extent by following Taylor's scientific approach to management in which he formulated four principles:

- The development of a true science of work.
  This principle relates to the fact that in some organizations no one knows what a fair day's work should be, this also applies to managers. As a result, confusion exists as to how much or how hard the workforce should work. This problem is eased, according to Taylor, if each person's daily task is established in terms of expected output. People are well paid if targets are met and fined if not.

- Scientific selection and training.
  In order for the workforce to earn their salary, employers must ensure that their staff are capable of doing their work both mentally and physically. Adequate and proper training must be given or received so that employees become 'first class' at their work.

- Bringing together the science of work and the trained man.
  Employees would be willing to co-operate in essential training if they knew what could be gained from doing so, such as, increased salary or promotion.

- The constant co-operation of management and staff.
  The various functions of an organization are divided amongst its employees. Managers in general provide instructions, specifications and supervision of work whilst the staff carry out instructions. If close personal co-operation is developed amongst the workforce, conflict is minimal, in that managers and the workers are subject to the same basic philosophy.

The above outlines some of the major contributions to management made by Taylor. He stressed the need of getting the right atmosphere and coined the term 'scientific management'. He demonstrated the values and importance of systematically analysing business operations so that efficiency is enhanced. From a practical point of view, many of Taylor's principles and ideas have much relevance for today's Leisure Managers. [28]

◆ FRANK B. GILBRETH (1868–1924) ◆

Gilbreth was another advocate of scientific management. He, along with his wife Lillian, was interested in motion or method study, the studying of the 'best' method of doing a job.

His research involved recording, observation and analysis of workers, equipment, materials and methods used in doing specific jobs. The work lead to other concepts such as time study and work study, more commonly known today as 'time and motion' studies.

The Gilbreths and Taylor were the first to develop motion study for purposes of industry. The former devised the name 'Therblig' (Gilbreth reversed) to denote several elements describing human motion. Such elements include: find, select, transport, grasp, empty, loaded, position, search and assemble. These factors were utilized to develop the rules of 'motion economy'.

◆ Motion economy ◆

Motion economy refers to the use of the human body to produce results with the least physical and mental effort. It has values to all professions including leisure management. Physiologists have also been involved with this concept and the following principles can apply as aids to getting a job done with minimum effort.

- ◆ Motions should be productive – Every motion a person makes should be focused on operations to bring a job closer to a finish. For example, the hands should not be wasted by holding the work, they should be released for more productive work.
- ◆ Motions should be simple – The fewer parts of the body used, the better, thus efforts become more economical.
- ◆ Motions should be rhythmical – Work should be arranged so that it is easy to work with smooth motions or actions.
- ◆ Make workers comfortable – The design of chairs, tools, and equipment should ensure the operator feels comfortable. This applies whether the operator has to sit, stand or move about to conduct his or her actions. This principle relates to the term 'ergonomics' which is the study of people in relation to their working environment, or fitting the job to the person so that more work with less effort is possible.
- ◆ Combine two or more tools – Picking up and laying down tools takes time. Less time is required if a tool has a working edge at either end or at the side.
- ◆ Pre-position tools and materials – This principle relates to having equipment and materials arranged and aligned before commencing a job, hence overall time is saved.
- ◆ Limit activity – Unnecessary actions waste time and effort, ultimately causing the onset of fatigue and poorer work performance.

- Use gravity when possible – Materials or waste can be fed by gravity through bins or chutes. This obviously reduces much time and energy loss.

The above principles have many practical values to the Leisure Manager. The extent depends, of course, on the type of leisure industry he or she is involved in.

◆ METHODS ENGINEERING ◆

The principles of motion economy described briefly above, led to the concept of methods engineering to cover an organized and scientific approach to developing effective working methods. The main objectives of methods engineering are listed below:

- To conserve worker's efforts.
- To conserve materials.
- To secure a properly balanced labour force.
- To secure maximum advantage from all mechanical aids to production.
- To improve quality.
- To make the maximum use of individual skills.
- To simplify further manufacture by means of simplification and standardization.
- To set up standards for control and incentives.

◆ ELTON MAYO (1880–1949) ◆

Mayo's main interest stemmed from the problems of tiredness at work, accidents and the high rate of staff turnover. He wanted to overcome, or reduce, these problems by changing the working environment, or by introducing 'rest' or 'break' intervals at work. Early theorists assumed that individual workers preferred to work in isolation and in pursuit of their own interest. The theories emanating from scientific management assumed that workers resembled machines so that they became more efficient.

Mayo and his co-workers became associated with the Western Electric Company at their plant in Hawthorne, Chicago. They conducted a series of experiments from 1927 to 1932, known as the Hawthorne experiments. Mayo began by acting on the assumptions made by scientific management principles.

The Hawthorne experiments made some very interesting discoveries about motivation. They could be regarded as a striking example of 'serendipity': the making of unexpected discoveries by accident or pure chance. Mayo and his colleagues wanted to measure the effect of changes in working conditions on the productivity of workers.

With regard to changes in light conditions, Mayo selected two similar groups of workers and kept a record of their output. He began by varying the intensity of lighting for one group whilst keeping the lighting constant for the other group. To Mayo's surprise, each time he changed the intensity of lighting either up or down, productivity increased, even when working conditions deteriorated from the change. It was later realized that unknown and unsuspected factors were upsetting the results of carefully planned 'scientific' experiments. Mayo made an important discovery about motivation. The group that continued to improve did so as a result of a whole set of factors that had nothing to do with lighting or illumination.

The very process of setting up experimental situations created social groups whose changes in attitude had gone unnoticed. Mayo discovered that the most significant factor was the social relationships which developed amongst the workers and their willingness to co-operate with management. The workers felt important because of the experiment and feedback: they became focuses of attention. Morale increased, work became more interesting and significant and productivity increased.

Advocates of Mayo's work are referred to as the 'Human Relation School'. The broad conclusions that can be derived from Mayo's experimental work at Hawthorne are:

- Work is a social or group activity.
- Workers generally react as members of a group or groups because the need for security and belonging is more important than the work environment itself.
- Informal groups exercise control over the way individuals work, think and act.
- Levels of work are not set by physical abilities alone, but by group attitudes.
- A human-relations approach enhances communication, participation and decision-making processes and improves efficiency and morale.

This approach opposes the scientific view that what is best for the company is also best for the workers (Taylor). By contrast, the human relations view suggests that what is best for the workers is best for the company and that the happiest firm (in terms of employee participation) is the most efficient.

The ideal for managers is to develop a balance between the two schools of thought. How this is to be achieved depends primarily on the individual manager's personality and leadership beliefs. Whichever approach is adopted, the various aims and objectives of the company should be met on a long-term basis.

◆ THE PETER PRINCIPLE ◆

Laurence Peter, a Canadian professor, discovered a rule in the business world which was universal and became known as the 'Peter Principle'. It began with a light-hearted study of occupational competence which subsequently became the subject of more serious debate.

The 'Peter Principle' states that bureaucratic systems promote people who are good at their jobs until they are finally promoted to do jobs they are not good at. In essence, therefore, employees tend to rise to their own level of incompetence until every post becomes occupied by an incompetent employee. Peter states that, 'In a hierarchy every employee tends to rise to his level of incompetence' or 'the cream rises until it sours' [29]. When posts are filled by incompetent employees, one may ask 'Who does the effective work?' Organizational collapse is only avoided because the work that has to be done is performed by those who have yet to reach their personal level of incompetence. It has been widely documented that executives and ambitious people striving for senior management positions are often victims of stress and associated illnesses such as ulcers, colitis, insomnia and cardiac inefficiency. Many people put these ailments down to the 'price of success'. Peter prefers to put them down to the 'price of incompetence'.

◆ QUALITY REQUIREMENTS ◆ FOR LEISURE MANAGERS

It is clear from the discussion above that management principles are diverse. Becoming conversant with the many principles is an aid to effective management, but more importantly, these have to be applied practically in the leisure environment. The extent to which this is done depends much upon the qualities, knowledge, experience and dedication a Leisure Manager possesses or acquires. The table below illustrates some of the qualities that are required in a Leisure Manager.

Manager	
Knowledge of job	Enthusiasm
Good health	Smart appearance
Knowledge of company policies	Creative ability
Reliable	Sociable
Acceptance of responsibility	Co-operative
Good communication skills	Articulate
Accuracy and honesty	Initiative
Vision and foresight	Able to delegate
Finance and budget skills	Marketing skills
Co-ordinator	Research ability
Adaptable and flexible	Leadership

Table 2   Some of the qualities required by a leisure manager

Achieving many of these qualities is a life-long process, meanwhile the duties and functions of a Leisure Manager still have to be conducted. With the vast range of qualities indicated, a similarly vast range of duties and responsibilities confront the Leisure Manager. These can be depicted diagrammatically in Figure 7.

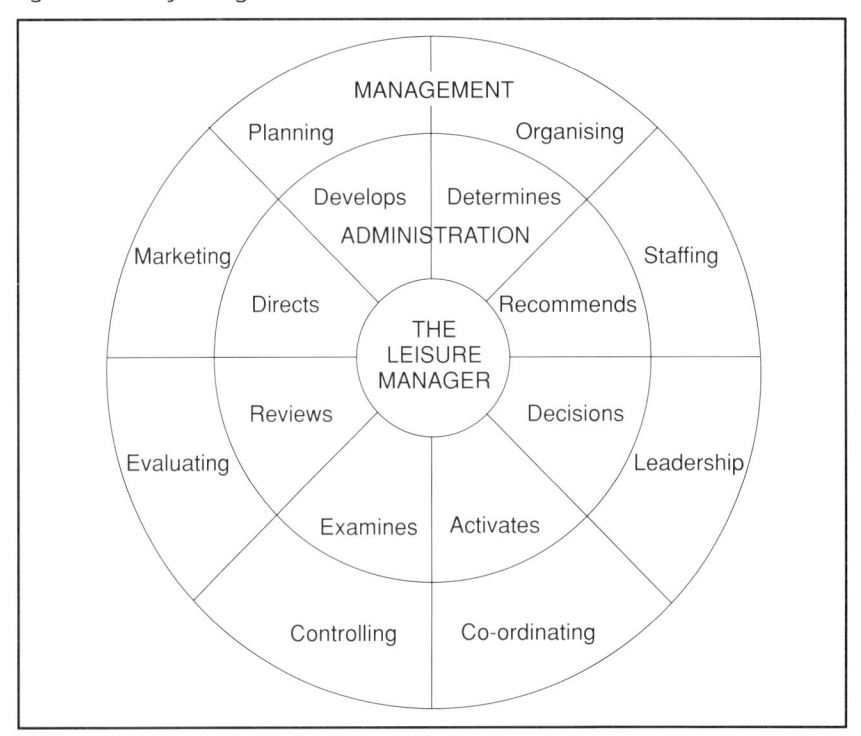

Fig. 7 The administrative and management functions of the Leisure Manager.

This section has focused on the requirements of Leisure Managers. Apart from these requirements, another important aspect for Leisure Managers to consider seriously is their responsibility towards staff. They have to decide on the special qualities they require from their recruits and on the provision of training necessary for further development of skills. Such considerations will enable the whole workforce to work effectively towards common goals.

While buildings, facilities and programmes are important in any enterprise, whether a financial company or a health and fitness club, there can be no more significant component of an organizational unit than the people in daily contact with the general public. Staff members in corporate, commercial and community settings will be the discriminating factor for the future success of the business. Unfortunately, some commercial clubs have yet to make the same financial investment in securing, training, and retaining quality staff as they do in providing bright new equipment set in well-lit and carpeted areas.

◆ Human resources ◆
management (Personnel management)

The people-orientated nature of the leisure business makes human resource management a high priority. Its goal is to recruit competent employees and provide the means for them to function to their optimum capacity. The problems of management are often most complex when dealing with the variability of human nature and behaviour, but the management of the personnel resources of any leisure or health and fitness organization is paramount to its success.

◆ Aspects of human resources management ◆

Some of the typical aspects of human resources management include:

- ◆ acquiring competent employees
- ◆ assigning them effectively
- ◆ motivating them to perform to their full potential
- ◆ stimulating their professional growth and development
- ◆ retaining or dismissing them.

The cost, in time and effort, of recruiting and training the new employee is substantial. The results of an unsuccessful selection can also be costly in terms of loss of productivity whilst a replacement is selected.

◆ Organizational charts ◆

All staffing selections should start with the administrative organizational chart. It should clearly illustrate the lines of authority and responsibility of the various members of the unit, by identifying the basic structure of the organization and where each employee fits into the scheme of the operation. The chart should be familiar to all employees and they should understand how their positions and duties contribute to the overall running of the unit.

◆ Recruitment ◆

This is an important managerial task. The wrong choice of employee could prove detrimental to a company's performance. A good manager will rarely delegate the process entirely. Close involvement in the selection procedure and liaison with the candidate establishes a sense of commitment between the two parties at an early stage. It is the philosophy of many organizations to look within the company to promote loyal and competent employees in preference to external recruitment. It is also a considerably cheaper method of filling a vacant position. This practice has the advantage of building staff morale and encouraging them to achieve a more desirable position. Internal recruitment also maintains the standard procedures of operation. External candidates may possess better qualifications and provide new ideas and approaches. A combination of externally and internally recruited employees is the preferred approach of most organizations.

◆ ORIENTATION ◆

To aid the assimilation of a new member of staff into the organization, some means of formal or informal training is required. The 'induction' process is allotted to a supervisor in many instances. Long-standing employees should be encouraged to help the new employee, correct minor errors, and be open to questions relating to the tasks expected of the newcomer.

Numerous positions in the leisure, health and fitness business require some on-the-job training to familiarize the new employee with equipment, machinery and/or facility operation. Specific plans to provide this knowledge and experience should be a part of this orientation process.

◆ CAREER DEVELOPMENT ◆

This should also exist for staff in any organization so that improvements and advancements can be made in the performance of the employee. Some organizations will offer opportunities free of charge or grant work-release for training. Other organizations may contribute towards the cost or merely encourage persons seeking advancement to acquire the additional skills. One of the trends in the health and fitness business is the need for employees to become familiar with computer technology. For example, many records, such as individual fitness profiles, inventories and financial accounts are now being computerized.

◆ STAFF APPRAISAL ◆

One of the most difficult tasks for managers is to appraise staff or give performance reviews. The reasons for assessing and appraising staff include the need to:

- ◆ maximize performance
- ◆ identify training needs
- ◆ provide data for salary and promotion reviews
- ◆ set targets for the future
- ◆ improve the understanding between the manager and his or her staff.

Employees are understandably sensitive about any official process of scrutiny because they feel their integrity or responsibility is being questioned. However, they need to have some idea of how effective they have been or whether more, or different, demands will be made of them.

A process of continuous review on an informal basis provides feedback on performance and prospects whilst simultaneously encouraging staff to practice self-appraisal. This approach will help a manager to judge his or her staff impartially without damaging team relationships. Job performance feedback is the primary use of appraisal information. Maier has described three approaches to appraisal feedback [30]:

- tell and sell
- tell and listen
- problem solving.

In the 'tell and sell' approach, the manager gives the appraisal information and reward decision to the employee. In the 'tell and listen' approach the manager listens to the employee's responses, but the comments are not used to adjust the performance appraisal or to begin a discussion of long-term matters such as training. Problem solving provides an opportunity for the manager and employee to discuss differences of opinion and explore opportunities for the employee's development and improvement. At the same time, the organization can benefit from the information employees share with their managers, for instance, their future plans, and their career aspirations.

DISCUSSION QUESTIONS

1. Distinguish between management and administration, giving examples relating to leisure management.

2. Discuss some of the processes involved in leisure management.

3. How important a part does planning and evaluation play in the management of leisure facilities?

4. Describe the qualities you consider important a Leisure Manager should possess or aim to achieve. Give reasons to support your answer.

5. Discuss the importance and significance of caring for your workforce or staff. What influence will this have?

◆ Case study ◆

The manager of Overseas Tours, Mr. J. Smithson, has been sick and off work for several weeks and his illness is likely to be long term. Since there is no appointed deputy, the staff are becoming increasingly frustrated because no one is prepared to make any serious decisions about the daily activities of the office. The present staff comprise of four junior and two longer serving receptionists and all work relatively independently.

The four junior receptionists met twice and decided to seek some way to improve the present situation in the office since they considered difficulties were worsening in Mr. Smithson's absence. They wanted to have some involvement in the decisions that personally affected them and wished to offer some practical advice that could be beneficial to all staff and the office functions as a whole.

The two longer serving receptionists took note of the juniors' views but stated categorically that they did not wish to intervene with senior management, fearing the loss of their jobs.

1. What problems do you see if no action is taken to improve the ongoing situation?

2. What difficulties do you think the office and business will develop if no positive measures are taken?

3. Discuss what you think should happen in the interest of the company.

TRENDS AND INFLUENCES IN THE HEALTH AND FITNESS BUSINESS

Few people would argue that there is not a fitness boom going on in the UK today. Fitness has become a way of life for a great number of people. With today's sedentary and automated life-styles, none of us can take good health and fitness for granted. The way to ensure a lifetime of physical well-being is regular participation in exercise and sports.

New products are being introduced daily to satisfy consumer demands. Similarly, there has been a large increase in various new journals and books arriving on the market. A significant percentage of the adult population is now regularly engaged in planned exercise. Most of these fitness enthusiasts are members of clubs or organizations that have facilities and equipment for participating in a wide variety of fitness and sports activities.

Health and fitness professionals are now being trained either through educational establishments or in–house management training offered by many organizations.

◆ SOME HEALTH AND ◆ FITNESS FACILITY CONSIDERATIONS

New technology, demographic changes, programme innovations, and consumers who are better informed and more demanding, lead to changes in health and fitness facilities.

If the manager is not upgrading, or planning to upgrade an existing facility, then undoubtedly, he or she will fall behind the competition and therefore, lose potential members as well as existing ones. It is imperative that a manager keeps up-to-date with facility design and construction either by means of literature or by seeking a good consultant when planning a new facility.

Some of these facility trends and influences are discussed below:

The business of health and fitness shows a clear trend in the specialization of space planning and architectural design. A manager will be well ahead of rivals if a good designer, specializing in health and fitness facilities is secured at the outset. Some firms provide a range of services from pre-design (feasibility, master planning), design, construction, personnel development and programme development to facility management. The architect identified in such firms is usually well acquainted with the special needs of health and fitness facilities.

The trend to develop multi-purpose facilities such as sports centres has replaced the single, or dual-purpose facilities popular in the early 1980s. Facility construction now requires a design that includes as much as possible in the way of recreation and fitness services. Many of the modern facilities in the corporate, commercial and community settings offer aquatic, squash, fitness and conditioning, open gym, and child care facilities. Some of these new facilities will undoubtedly offer additional outdoor recreational activities, inter-club leagues/competitions and excursion/travel trips to its members. A wide range of services will appeal to the broadest segment of the target market.

◆ SPECIFIC AREAS ◆

It is important to assess the types of users and what they want from a facility. The manager should consider important factors based on the information he has gathered, for example, the emphasis on easily cleaned materials, the imaginative use of colour to give a welcoming feeling to the user(s), the possibility of incorporating group changing and individual family areas. Such factors are becoming increasingly important as demand from schools and family units becomes more apparent. Security and privacy are also other important considerations.

◆ RECEPTION AND CONTROL ◆

The reception and control area is the client's first exposure to the facility. Members of the club or centre can 'book in' to the facility by desk-clerk recognition, membership card check, computer, or a combination of these methods.

The reception and control area also serves as an information centre for guests regarding facility guidelines and as a marketing tool for attracting new clients. For the members, it is a communication point where special events and announcements can be made or posted. The employees at the reception and control area should be the ambassadors of the health and fitness centre as well as acting as security control and should be highly skilled in both of these duties.

◆ Changing rooms and lockers ◆

Traditionally, changing rooms have been considered a purely functional item, a necessary part of the health and fitness club and one of the first areas targeted for cost-cutting. Today, this has changed. Changing rooms are much more flexible and attractive, reflecting the requirements of the user. Likewise, the locker area has undergone recent changes such as an enhanced environment, accomplished by well-placed, indirect lighting to create a pleasant ambience. The textured surfaces of the lockers are often wood veneer or some synthetic material, replacing the traditional ventilated metal storage locker. Carpets and good air-conditioning are a feature of the better clubs and centres.

Versatility of design, system and replacement are imperative and can have a big effect on perceived management standards.

◆ Shower facilities ◆

The choice and provision of shower facilities (that is, individual or communal) varies from centre to centre. Traditionally, communal showers were provided for men and individual showers for women. Nowadays, many centres provide individual showers for all adults and it is not unusual to see a communal shower for spillover purposes during peak usage of a centre, regardless of its prestige.

◆ General amenities ◆

Having amenity areas such as massage, equipment rental, sauna, tanning equipment, and catering services is a vital trend that often makes the difference between making a profit and a loss for the centre or club and enhances competition between clubs.

Within the corporate setting, amenities must be competitive with those of the commercial health and fitness centres or clubs. Most senior executives are also members of other centres or clubs and have come to expect the same or better level of amenities in their corporate fitness centres.

◆ Computer applications ◆

The health and fitness industry, like most businesses of today, can use computer technology to its advantage.

Computers are used in many health and fitness facilities to store an individual's fitness evaluation data, either as a record over the years or as a means of assisting the staff in the process of counselling, for example, on their dietary and exercise needs. This is aided by applying commercially available software to interact with the recorded data and instituting personal fitness regimes. The computer can also be used in data-base management for business applications. Many of the better known health and fitness software companies also supply business packages in their inventory of software. There are a number of business applications in the software inventories which include data-base management, word processing, and budget management. Most certainly, the age of the computer is upon us and therefore, those working in the leisure field should utilize its capabilities.

Developments in future computer applications are almost limitless. Some of the more conspicuous trends presenting themselves appear to be in the areas of voice recognition and voice simulation, coupled with artificial intelligence. Such advances would provide verbal exchanges between a computer system and an individual for example. The user friendliness of this innovation in computers would obviously heighten the capabilities of programmes and their operations.

A reliable forecast for future trends is interactive computerization. Imagine a scenario that allows members, on entering the reception and control area, to have their membership checked and their up-to-date fitness files called up by voice-activated computer terminals. Additionally, their cardiovascular training session could be pre-selected by a voice-activated unit on the exercise station of choice and the workload could be modulated at the prescribed level and duration. The data could then be converted to calories, stored, and eventually called up as a profile update for the member. It is obvious that adopting computers and their applications in the leisure field is necessary if a centre is to survive the competitive world of the 1990s.

◆ Equipment for cardiovascular performance ◆

The traditional gravity resisted bicycle ergometers, motor driven treadmills, and skipping ropes remain to the fore of cardiovascular exercise equipment. However, diversification is the trend similar to that in other areas. The introduction of the 'cardiovascular cross-training area' offers club members the chance to develop their exercise programme around the six main aerobic movements — cycling, treadmill, rowing, stepping, climbing and ski action. Undoubtedly, the list of new equipment will get longer as we continue to accommodate the consumer's demand for variety.

It is not uncommon to come across a variety of different approaches to the function of each type of equipment. For example, the bicycle ergometer can be bought with a variety of methods of work load production, monitoring, video feedback and microprocessor capabilities. With regard to work load production, examples include the gravity-resisted Monarch cycle, the electronic load-resistance cycle, the wind-resisted Airdyne cycle, and geared cycles that can be placed on rollers to produce variable resistance.

Bicycle ergometers can be bought either without monitoring facilities or with degrees of sophistication including monitored heart rates that can adjust work loads to accommodate a given target heart rate for a programmed period of time. Already there are units that have pre-programmed workloads which can produce interval, steady-state, or combination training periods that are preceded by warm-up and followed by cool-down periods.

◆ EQUIPMENT FOR STRENGTH AND POWER DEVELOPMENT ◆

Resistance-training equipment has the same growth and diversification as cardiovascular equipment. Traditional free-weights equipment, popular during the 1950s, went into decline during the 70s, as multi-station systems of rack-mounted weight plates developed. The recent progression to cam-loaded units such as Nautilus, and Powersport's powercam, together with the hydraulic and pneumatic units of recent times, have competed for the more demanding weight-training consumers. However, there has recently been a resurgence in the popularity of traditional free-weights units. Despite trends being generally driven by the influence of technology, it is difficult to replace a proven and successful strength-enhancing apparatus.

In most health and fitness clubs and centres today the trend is to provide a variety of training and conditioning methods. Expected trends will be linked to technological developments in fitness equipment. The continued use of electronics incorporated into the product will also occur.

◆ FACILITIES FOR SWIMMING ◆

There are a few exciting innovations emerging in facilities for swimming, the most prominent being the variable-level floor, which is routinely adjustable. Having such a facility allows a wide variety of swimming programmed for all age levels and, importantly, it allows disabled people entry without the requirement of a hoist. Separated air currents over the water surface and the walking/lounging surfaces to accommodate the need for varied humidities and temperatures in these areas, is another innovation.

A very popular introduction, especially to young people, has been the miniaturised flume. Any club which has space problems or budget restrictions and therefore cannot provide for a pool, may find the answer in the miniflume. A committed swimmer can enter a deep, 3 metre long bathtub-type structure and turn on adjustable water jets to prevent travelling any horizontal distance whilst swimming in the flume. This idea is similar to a treadmill, fairly inexpensive and space conserving, and gives the committed swimmer an opportunity to train in a club that does not possess an olympic-sized pool. However, nearly all of these 'water treadmills' are in the USA and have yet to stand the test of time.

◆ Squash courts ◆

Squash remains one of the more popular sports played despite a slight decline in the number of participants. Recent enhancements to the game of squash have included glass walls, especially in competition courts where spectators can view the game and its players. This development has also helped the game of squash to secure TV sponsorship, which is important for the game and its elite players.

Attempts have been made to convert courts that are not fully utilised to small free-weights areas. The court can be arranged to ensure security as well as isolation for the committed lifters away from the recreational weight trainers. The move towards multi-purpose facilities has placed the burden of change on the single-purpose club undergoing financial pressures.

◆ Aerobics and keep fit activity areas ◆

Aerobic classes have, until recently, been taught in a multi-purpose gym or hall. However, the aerobics studio is an extremely important area in any health and fitness centre or club and the sound system requirements have necessitated acoustical engineering and structural adjustments such as changes to the floor surface so that impact-related injuries to the aerobics performer are reduced. Floors constructed from spring-loaded hardwood are presently favoured as one of the best surfaces, closely followed by heavily padded carpet surfaces that are sealed and bonded with plastic laminate, to prevent moisture penetration below the pile textures.

Further steps to prevent injuries in aerobics include the introduction of low– or no–impact aerobic classes. A move towards providing rhythmical exercise classes against a background of upbeat contemporary music, is popular amongst people who want to enjoy the creative and social dimensions of exercise. The appeal of rhythmical exercise will remain although its manifestations continue to change and evolve.

A good aerobics facility will have a raised platform allowing a clear view of the instructor. In addition the platform can provide a convenient space for other keep fit activities or meetings and behavioural programming such as nutrition, weight control and exercise, smoking cessation, low back pain management, stress management and relaxation classes. The only requirement in such an area is a small storage area for stacked chairs and mats etc. Limited financial resources and stiff competition from other centres necessitates maximum usage of an available space.

◆ GYMNASIA ◆

The subject of gymnasia is only discussed briefly in this text. A reader seeking further information should consult relevant sources. The nature and large space of a gymnasium must be put to use in a variety of ways to make it cost-effective and efficient. For example a single gym floor could be used during the day for basketball, volleyball, tennis and indoor soccer, as well as all the functions performed in the aerobics studio, if an alternative area is unavailable. An area as large and diverse as a gymnasium requires effective and efficient lighting suitable for all activities. Low pressure sodium lighting with its superior performance at lower cost is the popular choice.

◆ OUTDOOR FACILITIES ◆

Discussion will again be limited to just a few areas that directly affect health and fitness programming. Most leisure centres and clubs will have a 'greenbelt' area that serves a dual purpose of creating an attractive and inviting environment and providing jogging, cycling and trim trails for physical activity. Areas such as these, are generally surfaced with an all-weather composition and have strategically placed exercise stations around the path. Planned flexibility and warm-up stations, vital for the prevention of injury, are generally added to the circuit as well for use prior to vigorous exercise. The addition of outdoor facilities creates variety to a fitness and conditioning programme as well as providing additional options for the user.

◆ PLANNING AND THE PROVISION ◆ OF HEALTH AND FITNESS PROGRAMMES

Planning is the process of arranging the various elements of a programme in order to obtain constructive and worthwhile results. Effective planning and organization can help attain immediate goals and determine long range objectives. The objective of programme planning is primarily to provide satisfaction to the participant in terms of fitness, whilst simultaneously providing a social venue. Health and fitness leaders must organize and conduct activities in a manner that will accomplish this major objective.

Planners should have a course of action: a plan to follow. A well trained professional staff which is creative, enthusiastic and sensitive to user needs is the key ingredient in a successful health and fitness programme.

◆ FITNESS TESTING ◆

Fitness testing is a form of physical examination. It usually involves physical activity and hence the question often asked is, 'can it be dangerous?'

Astrand, the famous Swedish exercise physiologist, says:

> 'The question is frequently raised whether a medical examination is advisable before commencing a fitness training programme. Certainly anyone who is doubtful about his state of health should consult a physician. In principle, however, there is less risk in activity than in continuous inactivity. In a nut shell, our opinion is that it is more advisable to pass a careful medical examination if one intends to be sedentary in order to establish whether one's state of health is good enough to stand the inactivity' [31].

For those under 35 years of age, with no obvious health risk (e.g. high blood pressure, a history of heart disease, overweight, diabetes mellitus), a fitness test serves both as motivation and to check on progress at a later stage. For others, it might be useful as a screening device, and to help devise a programme to suit special needs.

It is now appropriate to discuss some of the programme provisions for those in the health and fitness field.

◆ THE 'WELLNESS' MOVEMENT ◆

There have been many innovations in health and fitness programming. One of the most prominent has been the 'wellness' movement, or the move from exercise and fitness related services only, towards an holistic health service. Such health services include nutrition, weight control, stress management, substance-abuse control, and low back pain management. 'Wellness' programmes are usually preceded by an appraisal of health risk or health behaviour. As soon as the individual's net score is known in the various assessment areas, then counselling and programming is directed towards his or her needs and interests.

◆ SPECIAL EVENTS ◆

Fun runs, group travel excursions, and special events related to ability and interest are just a few activities that are extremely popular with the general public. It is important to bear in mind that all of these special events develop 'togetherness' and renewed interest amongst the participants and encourage new membership.

◆ SPECIAL INTEREST GROUPS ◆

Programme modification is another avenue of meeting the needs of special interest groups. For example, a brisk walking group for the over-50s could be added and carefully monitored, to encourage participation and cater for their fitness needs. It is worth considering any modification to a regular programme if it will attract interest from a wider cross-section of members. An option of this sort will improve a centre or club's chances of survival in the face of financial or competitive constraints.

◆ FAMILY TARGETING ◆

Programmes must be dynamic and constantly up-dated to take into account new demands, changing needs and new opportunities for people. Many fitness leaders (and leisure managers) will say that their club or centre is full to capacity already. A static programme loses its impetus, becomes stagnant and, in the long term, poorer for all.

Family involvement is such an example of a modern programme. Crêche and nursery services have sprung up in clubs and centres to attract and allow women to participate in many different fitness activities. Special weekend-time periods during which adult members can bring the entire family to the club or centre for events exclusively scheduled for them, are proving to be popular. Encouraging the entire family for lifetime fitness and health will be, and is, a definite priority.

◆ SPECIAL MARKET PROGRAMMES ◆

There are a number of health and fitness clubs and centres which are being creative in their services so as to attract the many different markets within the population. For instance, there are a number of programmes today, that cater for a personal exercise trainer to work alongside each individual member, even though it is an expensive service. In addition, there are a few creative individuals who have started offering this service to clients at their own homes or workplaces. By using a van equipped with all the exercise equipment, the instructor can visit the client and offer a personalized programme of fitness.

◆ GUIDELINES FOR CHOOSING, BUYING ◆ AND MAINTAINING EXERCISE EQUIPMENT

The choosing, buying, maintenance and operation of exercise equipment is all part of an extremely important aspect of the health and fitness business. Time taken to choose equipment is time well spent in view of the potential financial investment. Hasty decisions can be costly in the long term. A wide range of products, of various prices are available on the market and the buyer is faced with a bewildering array of health and fitness equipment to choose from. Looking at classified advertisements in trade journals and visiting trade show exhibitions will certainly baffle all but a few professionals who spend many hours dealing in such matters. We now discuss some *guidelines* for making a sound choice of equipment.

◆ SAFETY ◆

The safety aspect of any piece of equipment is the first priority when considering the purchase of health and fitness equipment. You have a responsibility to provide a reasonably injury-free environment for those people taking part in exercise. Always check the weight machines, free weights, and the cardiovascular equipment plus any other major equipment on a daily basis. If you cannot perform this yourself, give another staff member the responsibility.

◆ SPACE ◆

The amount of space required or available often determines the type and/or amount of equipment chosen in a health and fitness club or centre. In designing exercise spaces, a rule of thumb is that one station of exercise equipment takes up approximately 46 square feet of floor space. This takes into account the movement of participants and averages the space for both larger items (e.g. treadmills) and smaller items (e.g. bicycle ergometers) including large weight racks and single-function units. If the facility is planned only for multi-functional unit of equipment such as a 12 station Universal Gym, the above assumptions are removed. In this case, you should consult the vendor. It is important to bear in mind that many manufacturers of exercise equipment provide space planning services that are of paramount importance in the space planning process, especially if you are planning to employ only one brand of equipment.

Plan for as many exercise patterns in one space as possible to optimise the utilization of space. To give an example, design a circuit on Nautilus equipment around a group of ergometers to accommodate a super-circuit if a participant is eager to train in both areas simultaneously.

◆ FUNCTION ◆

Exercise equipment is generally designed for a particular function or purpose. For example, a bicycle ergometer is designed to function as an exercise station for the development of cardiovascular endurance and free weights (bar and attached weights) are designed mainly to develop muscular strength and endurance. However, most equipment can be modified or adapted to accomplish secondary functions. For instance, free weights equipment can be modified to a low resistance allowing a high number of exercise repetitions aimed at promoting cardiovascular endurance. Therefore studying the variety of functions a piece of equipment performs, is an important task.

Basic questions in the early stages of decision-making will include the kind of image to be conveyed, who will be using the equipment, what is the main purpose of the equipment, and will the emphasis be on strength or endurance equipment? Questions such as these, can only be answered, if a clear plan of action has been laid down.

◆ VERSATILITY ◆

Each piece of equipment must be able to perform more than one function hence versatility is extremely important when buying health and fitness equipment. For instance, the equipment should be capable of identifying a participant's fitness capacity, rehabilitating injury, or training the injury-free member of the club or centre. Furthermore, the exercise equipment should be reliable so that the same information is acquired on the same subject in repeated tests. Accuracy is also important, in that it should measure what the test is designed for, for example, using a treadmill may best measure running ability. Also, the equipment should provide objectivity in that the same results should be obtained when two different people test a participant.

A further consideration is to check whether the equipment can be modified for different populations. For example, can either the young or women or men use the same piece of equipment effectively? If this is not possible, then it is in your interests to find alternative equipment that has versatility of usage.

◆ DURABILITY ◆

The durability of the proposed equipment is an important factor to consider. No formula exists to calculate the useful life expectancy of exercise equipment in a club or centre. A particular type of equipment may last longer in some settings than it does in others. Some points to consider are:

- ◆ the user will often change his or her preferences for equipment. For example, the exerciser may go from one type of exercise equipment to another in pursuit of the quickest and biggest gain.
- ◆ new equipment will at first attract intense periods of heavy usage eventually dwindling to periods of little or no use.

The equipment warranty is a good indicator of the life expectancy of equipment. For instance, manufacturers of strength-enhancing equipment generally warranty the structure frame for life and the moving parts for a year.

Obviously each item has a different projected life span. Always pay particular attention to the small print in a warranty that undertakes a lifetime guarantee. Manufacturers are extremely careful to extend a warranty to customers that will require extremely low repair activity at their expense. Assume that expected deterioration rates of equipment under normal conditions will exceed the warranty period advertised by the manufacturer.

A further indicator of durability is to examine your main competitor's experiences with the equipment. An evaluation such as this, coupled with trade journal commentary, should provide the necessary information to make the right decision about exercise equipment durability.

◆ Price ◆

Exercise equipment can vary from anything from a few pounds to several thousand pounds with little difference in performance. For example, a high-tech computerized product may look more impressive than a dumbell (available for only a few pounds) yet provide the same function at much greater expense.

The difference is one of sophistication involved in the measurement of an individual's fitness. The computerized product might, for example, provide concentric and eccentric workouts in variable modes such as pyramid or a maximal effort routine. When choosing equipment always be extremely careful. There is the possibility of a point of diminishing returns when older equipment is upgraded for newer products. The price of equipment can put a programme in financial difficulty and a burden on the budget, so that other important areas such as personnel, might have to be sacrificed. Both equipment and quality personnel are highly visible marketing tools and as a result, a balance of expenditure is of paramount importance.

Payment is normally demanded prior to, or at the time of delivery. Although delivery dates are often extended from 4 to 8 weeks, a large expenditure of money over short periods of time can be a burden. Alternatives to buying new equipment outright, should be considered.

Buying used equipment is one alternative. Phone calls to the chosen equipment manufacturer may reveal the option of a trade-in deal. Another alternative to buying new equipment is to recondition the used equipment. A number of companies can restore old equipment to virtually new condition and save the centre a considerable financial outlay.

On commencing a new business venture, a combination of used and new equipment is worth considering. Placing the new equipment in a prominent position can be advantageous and give the general impression that all equipment is brand new but ideally this scheme should only be employed when an investor is seeking an early break-even period and a swift return on his or her investment and not prolonged unnecessarily. A lease or a lease/purchase arrangement is yet another possibility. These arrangements, again, can be attractive to investors who are impatient for quick returns on their investment.

♦ MAINTENANCE ♦

Many manufacturers provide service contracts especially at the time of purchase. Purchasers without repair personnel, should consider this option. A maintenance contract will enhance the promotion of safety and advertise the equipment's durability.

Once the equipment has been bought, the endless process of maintenance commences. Two hundred to 400 people daily using health and fitness facilities will obviously cause stress to the equipment. Improper maintenance will render the equipment unsafe and shorten its life span.

Finally, internal maintenance of equipment (including cleaning) is very important, because it limits the amount of external service needed and delays expensive breakdowns. It is imperative that cleanliness is adhered to in the health and fitness club or centre and should be an ongoing and well organized process.

♦ TRENDS AND FUTURE MARKETS ♦ IN THE HEALTH AND FITNESS BUSINESS

Trends develop rapidly and there are a number of forces acting on the health and fitness business that will have a major influence on its direction in the future. These influences include the increase of participation by the 'mature' age group. Perhaps the most dramatic change has been the growing interest amongst older people, especially the over-50s, in a wide range of activities including health related activities — fitness training, jogging, aerobics, running and weights; indoor bowls and dance; informal countryside activities — rambling and orienteering; a 'veterans' boom — rowing, 'Golden Oldies' in Rugby Union, Masters' Swimming; other sports which traditionally survive into middle age — badminton and swimming.

Figure 8 shows changes in the age structure projected for 1993–2003. Even though the forecast for the increase in population is by only 400,000 (0.8%) before 1993, there will be significant changes in the age structure. The 25–44 age group is projected to increase by 500,000 (4%) and the 45–59 age group by 600,000 (8%) by 1993. The latter group will continue to grow after 1993.

The projected decrease of 1 million (15%) in the 16–24 age group (traditionally the largest number of participants), is of great importance to leisure, sports and fitness agencies. This trend will continue but at a slower rate, after 1993. The leisure industry will be required to adjust to these demographic changes, placing emphasis on growth areas such as the 'mature' market, in order to overcome losses in declining areas. Team and strength-based sports, traditionally catered for and performed by the young may decline. Health supporting activities which also involve an element of socializing may turn out to be more attractive.

The mature market increase will create a real need for trained professionals and upgraded facilities for this large segment of our society.

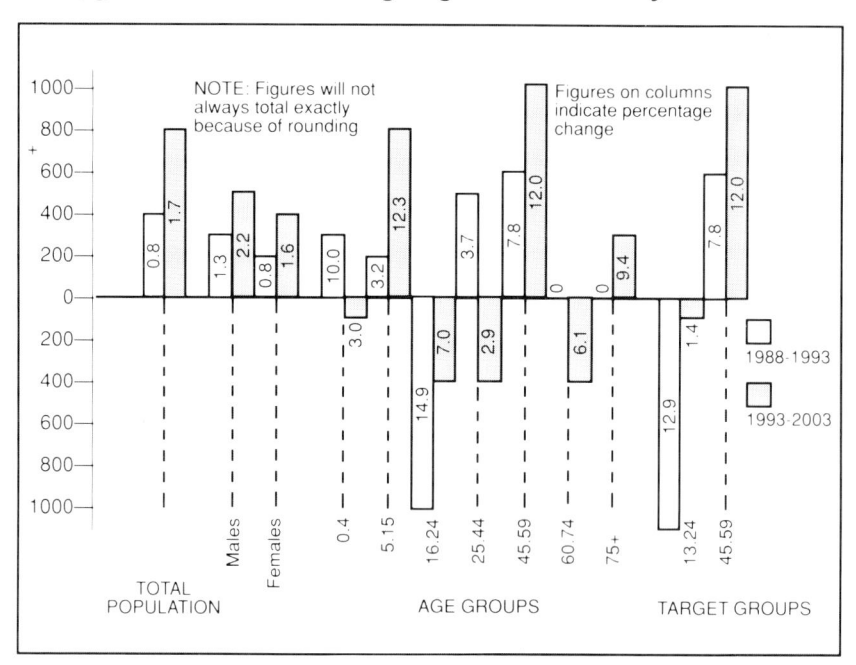

Fig. 8 Projected changes in the age structure of the English population 1993 - 2003
Source: Office of Population censuses and surveys, 1985, 1983-2023 Population Projections, Microfiche, Series PP2, No. 13

◆ HIGH-TECHNOLOGY PROGRAMMES ◆

High technology will continue to affect our health and fitness programmes in many ways. In some instances technology has already outstripped the capabilities of staff. For instance, the computerized card readers for checking in to the facility, the interactive computer programmes available for prescription and programming, and the management software programmes. Management must therefore, attempt to bridge the gap between the technology available and the services delivered by the staff.

◆ HOTELS ◆

A particular growth area in leisure is the hotel industry. People now expect to continue their keep-fit lifestyle when they travel for business or pleasure.

Health and fitness facilities in hotels are becoming an important marketing tool.

The decade ahead will certainly offer a variety of challenges to those in the leisure services field, but as Sessons (1989) pointed out:

> 'The degree to which we meet those opportunities will depend largely upon the actions we take now in conceptualizing who we are, what we can and should do, and how we go about meeting our task.' [33]

◆ DISCUSSION QUESTIONS ◆

1. What programmes or services in your community are contributing to the fitness boom?

2. Indicate the value to be derived from special events programming in the health and fitness business.

3. Does the health and fitness motivation for sport participation change for older adults? How much fitness activity is aimed more towards appearance than health?

4. The choosing, buying, maintenance and operation of exercise equipment are all important parts of a very important process in the health and fitness profession. Why?

◆ CASE STUDY ◆

A job advert appears in a leisure management magazine and contains the following information:

Wholesome Leisure are currently assembling their management team for a network of high quality health and fitness clubs. The first will open shortly in the City of London and requires dynamic individuals to operate the most advanced health and fitness clubs in the country. Further London clubs are scheduled to open later on.

The Wholesome Leisure Club at the White City contains an unparalleled range of fitness, medical and relaxation facilities with outstanding opportunities for the ambitious employee. Positions available:

1. *Fitness Director*
   Extensive experience in managing exercise facilities is essential, including an involvement with sports medical facilities. Relevant academic qualifications will be required. It would also be advantageous if the candidate could predict future trends that are likely to emerge as a result of the impact of present conditions on the profession.

2. *Class Co-ordinator*
   Experience in designing and implementing a high quality schedule of classes and programmes is essential.

3. *Fitness Instructor*
   The successful candidate will require exercise prescription experience and relevant qualifications.
   We are looking for creative and enthusiastic individuals who are self-motivated and work well within a busy, lively team of professionals. Commitment to excellence is essential.
   Written replies only to:
   The General Manager
   Wholesome Leisure Club
   2 The Avenue
   White City
   London EC4 7PR
   You are interested in one of the posts and wish to apply urgently.

Choose one of the vacant posts and prepare a CV and covering letter for the general manager giving details of your experience, knowledge and commitment to the health and fitness field. Mention your predictions for the future concerning your chosen job application.

JOINT PROVISION AND DUAL USE OF FACILITIES FOR SPORT AND RECREATION

*T*he concepts of joint provision and dual use have been the subject of focus for several years, but more recently, their roles for the leisure industry have become increasingly important. Great financial saving can be made, whilst, at the same time offering a broad range of facilities and activities when such schemes are implemented. Many local authorities and private agencies realize these benefits and are encouraged to operate these schemes for new developments or when undergoing reorganization.

The implementation and management of these schemes calls for many managerial and administrative skills. Therefore, it is apt to dwell on the various applications and implications that are inherent in both joint provision and dual use schemes.

◆ JOINT PROVISION ◆

The East Midlands Sports Council, states that:

> *'Joint provision involves co-operation on the part of two or more authorities in the joint planning and provision of facilities. Usually it is an education authority and/or a local authority and voluntary body which combine resources to provide and manage a facility to be used by school and public to the mutual advantage of all parties' 1980.*

A North West Sports Council Report defines joint provision thus:

> *'where facilities have been jointly provided by separate departments (or authorities) to meet the needs of both schools and community; the end product is the same' 1982.*

The Northern Region Sports Council consider joint provision to mean:

> *'the sharing of facilities planned and designed from the outset to accommodate both school and community use — or use jointly by two or more providing agencies' 1987.*

Finally, the House of Lords Report, on sport and recreation state that joint provision:

> *'usually involves the co-operation of two or more authorities in the joint planning and provision of facilities. Generally it is an education authority*

and a local authority who combine in a dual provision scheme to provide facilities which will be used by school and public and which will be better than either authority could afford individually' 1973.

It is clear from the above sources, that joint provision essentially involves a partnership of two or more agencies involving, in the main, schools and community. Another important point worthy of consideration and noted in the House of Lords Report above, is that the facilities provided by joint provision would be more extensive than either party could afford individually.

◆ Dual use ◆

According to the Sports Council dual use is:

'The long-term regular use, on an organised basis, of facilities, particularly those financed from public funds, by the general public, either as members of groups or clubs or as individuals, for whom the facility was not primarily intended' 1982.

Dual use according to the Sports Council Northern Region: 'implies access to existing facilities and the focus of attention is chiefly on school-based facilities' 1987.

Sometimes the term 'dual use' is used to refer to the difference between local residents and visitors to the area. Many towns and cities have attractions of historical interest which draw people from different parts of the country and abroad, these are used by visitors and locals alike. Hence, the concept of dual use may involve more than school children and the local community. A similar distinction applies at seaside resorts.

Terms such as: 'multi-purpose', 'dual provision', 'multi-use', 'joint use' and 'joint planning' are also in use. They are discussed briefly in order to avoid any uncertainties or ambiguities.

MULTI-PURPOSE facilities can cater for more than one activity. For example, a sports hall could be used for conferences, exhibitions, banqueting and craft shows as well as a range of sporting activities. Multi-purpose facilities, therefore, can provide or facilitate for multi-use activities.

JOINT PLANNING is the coming together of two or more groups in designing and utilizing a facility for mutual benefit.

DUAL PROVISION, is:

'The integrated planning of facilities for educational establishments and for the community so that each facility is augmented and improved to the mutual benefit of all users' the Sports Council (1982).

◆ BACKGROUND DEVELOPMENT OF ◆ JOINT PROVISION AND DUAL USE

The concepts of joint provision and dual use date back many years to when it was first realized that financial advantages could be gained from the dual use of existing facilities.

Swimming pools during the 1930s and 1940s were used for dual purposes, especially during the winter months when heating was expensive. The pools were drained and covered with boards at deck level so that dancing and other activities could take place.

For many years private companies and industries have provided leisure facilities for their employees in the form of sport and social clubs. Some of these companies have also adopted the principles of dual use, not only to make their facilities more widely available, but also as a means of generating income through rental or hiring schemes when the facilities are not being used by their own members.

Community schools first appeared through developments made in Cambridgeshire during the 1930s and Leicestershire during the 1950s. These developments centred on secondary schools in small villages and towns where alternative facilities were considered lacking. Such developments enhanced the opportunities for individuals to fulfil their leisure potential and aspirations in the form of club, family or individual participation.

In 1964, a joint circular from the Department of Education and Science (DES) and the Ministry of Housing and Local Government entitled, *Provision of Facilities for Sport*, highlighted the measures the government was taking to encourage the future development of sport and suggested ways in which local authorities could co-operate with voluntary and other interested bodies to improve and extend facilities in their areas for children and the community. The circular also pointed out the many advantages and possibilities of using funds from voluntary and local authority sources. This would allow for schools to enjoy better facilities and opportunities than could otherwise have been provided solely from the DES. Likewise, the local community would also share such enhanced facilities and opportunities for increased participation.

The joint circular had a major influence on several local education authorities. For example, important changes took place during 1965 at Egremont comprehensive school in Cumbria. Design modifications were made to integrate the facilities of the school, public library and community leisure centre.

This was followed shortly by Nottinghamshire, where the physical education departments of four comprehensive schools were modified jointly with district councils to develop dual use facilities. In 1969 Bingham comprehensive school was developed jointly by Rushcliffe Borough Council and the County Council for dual use purposes. This set the standard and pattern for other developments at the Carlton Forum, Newark and Worksop, in addition to other schemes throughout the country.

These early schemes proved successful and had a major impact on future social planning and on the co-ordination of local authority housing, education and recreation policies. The basic principle of combining different sources of funding to support joint provision and dual use stimulated the publication of many government reports and circulars.

The DES circular, *A Chance to Share*, granted local authorities more control over local expenditure for sport and recreation schemes and encouraged developments for music, craft and drama facilities. The House of Lords Report (1973), argued that numerous benefits could be derived from dual use and dual provision (later to become known as joint provision). The Report regarded dual use to be:

> *'the most important answer to the shortage of sports and social facilities within the community. Schools and Colleges should be recognised as an investment by the community for the community, and the more that they are integrated the better it should be for schoolchildren and the public'.*

The 1975 White Paper by the Department of Environment entitled, *Sport and Recreation*, stressed the economic difficulties that may arise from the provision of new facilities or the better utilization of existing facilities. It favoured sharing facilities indicating that, 'It is wrong if good and expensive facilities are underused'.

The West Midlands Sports Council noted the comments of both the 1973 House of Lords Report and the 1975 White Paper in their document, *Dual Use of Education Facilities*. They also made a pertinent note that: 'In a period of financial restraint in particular, it is important to ensure that the maximum use is made by the community of facilities already available'.

The development of joint provision and dual use gained momentum during the 1970s, but by 1980, the emergence of the private sector began to have an effect. The much admired Aston Villa Recreation Centre became possible through the co-operation between the City of Birmingham, Aston Villa Football Club, the Sports Council and the Asda Supermarket chain. This initiative lead to other developments which extended beyond sport. The twelve Regional Arts Associations of England have also adopted the principles of joint provision and dual use with funds from such sources as local authorities, local education authorities, the Arts Council and the commercial sector.

In March 1980, the East Midlands Sports Council paper, *Sport and Recreation on School Facilities*, highlighted the fact that the major objective of joint provision and dual use should be:

> 'to secure optimum use of plant, buildings and other resources, in seeking to meet the growing sporting and recreational needs of the community'.

This was followed by an in-depth study entitled *Sharing Does Work* (1981), reporting on the economic and social benefits and costs of direct and joint sports provision. The study made four main assumptions:

(a) Sharing is the most economic way to provide sport and leisure facilities on the assumption that they can be planned ahead of time.
(b) Sharing allows for a more extensive or better quality sports facilities than could be provided by either a recreation or an education authority individually.
(c) Sharing prevents expensive capital plant from lying idle, given that, in any case, schools must supply some sport facilities.
(d) A joint provision facility (particularly when it is a school) is likely to become useful to the rest of the community as a nucleus of recreation activities.

The study also produced evidence that joint provision is almost twice as cost-effective as a separate provision. Its main results appear in Table 3 but do not unfortunately give any indication of the range of results within any one type or size of facility.

Type of centre	Type of control	Cost-effectiveness (i.e. visits : operating costs)
All	Joint	2 : 7
	Separate	1 : 5
Dry	Joint	4 : 9
	Separate	1 : 5
Wet & Dry	Joint	2 : 1
	Separate	1 : 5
Small	Joint	3 : 3
	Separate	1 : 4
Medium	Joint	1 : 7
	Separate	1 : 7
Large	Joint	3 : 2
	Separate	1 : 3

Table 3 Cost-effectiveness in joint and separately provided sports centres, UK, 1981

Source: Coopers & Lybrand, 1981 [57]

The study concluded that:

> 'the economical and financial arguments for joint provision and dual use are so strong that it is surprising to find that the majority of facilities are still provided and operated on a separate basis, though conflicts over policy objectives and administration may help to explain this'.

The last words indicate that serious thought must be given to administration procedures when contemplating the implementation of a joint provision or dual use scheme.

Sharing does work was closely followed by the Sports Council's *Sport and the Community — The Next Ten Years* (1982). It gave clear and positive guidelines to using dual use facilities and also indicated the rapid increase in leisure facilities and spending.

Further initiatives continued for the encouragement and development of joint provision and dual use schemes. A joint initiative between the Sports Council and the Department of Environment (1984), highlighted the problem that too many educationally funded buildings closed or were underused outside educational operating hours and the Eastern Council for Sport and Recreation, in their document, *Dual Use — Turning Policies into Practice* (1987) recommended that: 'Action should be taken to identify and make use of 'spare capacity' during the evenings, weekends and school holidays'.

Another Report from the Sports Council of Wales (1988), suggests that:

> 'Joint provision and optimum use represents excellent value for money ... Through such projects recreational opportunities are more widely available to the public at large and at a cost which can be afforded by all but the severely disadvantaged. In essence, it is a most effective means of increasing opportunity and bringing closer to reality the "Sport for All" concept'.

From the above discussion, it is evident that the concepts of joint provision and dual use have been in existence for several years with a steady flow of reports and documents. Although these have mostly emphasised benefits the drawbacks must also be discussed. The following sections will briefly outline the various advantages and disadvantages of both joint provision and dual use.

◆ ADVANTAGES OF JOINT ◆ PROVISION AND DUAL USE FACILITIES

- ◆ Economic savings — The pooling of resources and fundings for joint schemes in the provision of leisure opportunities, allows for greater financial viability than is possible from a single source of income. This, in effect, creates a lower capital expenditure and sharing of running or on-going costs. Additionally, a partnership approach to joint planning, can allow an authority to offer several centres on a neighbourhood basis, as in the case of Nottinghamshire discussed in the previous section. A greater degree of cost-effectiveness is achieved through joint schemes than would be in individual schemes.

Another approach to joint provision with possible economic rewards is for the co-operation between two authorities to provide one large centre ('integrated facilities') which would otherwise not be possible. For example, Manchester's Abraham Moss Centre, is run in conjunction with a comprehensive school, college of further education and a youth centre. It also has integrated facilities with a library, recreation centre and social and community centres.

◆ Improved facilities — The range and quality of facilities can be improved enormously by joint provision. School children and the general public derive numerous benefits in the quality of their education through enhanced facilities.

◆ Increased participation — Greater usage of facilities and participation is fostered through joint provision for a variety of reasons. For example, children and school staff are likely to participate more frequently through ease of access to the facilities. These people, along with the general public, may be more tempted to try new sports that are offered locally, and children, in particular, may be encouraged to continue leisure or sporting activities in the evenings.

Joint provision attempts to foster maximum participation, since it is considered unjust to under-use good public facilities, especially in the light of escalating costs in land and buildings. By encouraging greater participation throughout the year and beyond the school day, enormous savings can be made along with generating income.

◆ Skill development — Many schools have benefitted from the high quality of facilities that joint provision and dual use schemes offer, along with the range of activities they permit. The enhanced facilities allow for improvements in standards of performance and achievement in a range of physical skills. Some schools have had the opportunity to provide excellent training and competition facilities. Joint provision schemes are particularly welcomed by physical education (PE) and other teaching staff who recognize the fact that high standards of skill development and performance could not be achieved with reduced levels of facilities in terms of their quality and range.

◆ Social development — Increased participation levels help towards social development by bringing more people together to share common interests within pleasant environments. The harmony of schools and communities that these schemes help to foster, plays a vital role in today's society by promoting participation across the whole age spectrum, hence uniting the community more fully.

◆ Wider range of staff expertise — Joint provision and dual use schemes bring together a broad range of staff whose experiences and expertise will be diverse. This diversity of skills permits broader programmes and better utilization of facilities to the benefits of all users.

◆ Meeting people's demands — With the continued increase in people's leisure time, greater demands are made on Leisure Managers to cater for a more diverse range of activities. Joint provision and dual use help towards meeting these demands. They offer several opportunities for expansion if existing facilities are over-subscribed.

Joint provision and dual use schemes can respond quite quickly to changes in people's leisure demands and also adapt sharply to relatively short-lived activities, for example, skate boarding. These rapid adaptations to people's demands rest essentially on the flexibility of the facility design and the ability of Leisure Managers to anticipate, predict and respond to such changes. Torkildsen (1987), outlines several categories of people with varying needs which could be met in joint provision and dual use schemes.

People	Possible expectations
Recreational user	a pleasant environment to play and meet
High standard user	specific sports requirements
Older user	active and passive pursuits, warmth, a social setting
Young adults	novelty, adventure, noise, play, social needs, youth culture
Parent/housewife	daytime activities; somewhere for children, not just a crèche for infants but play opportunity for young children
Manager and staff	functional and attractive centre; facilities grouped to assist management, supervision and communication; designs which make it easy to maintain
Mayor and councillors	a centre which the council can be proud of, which meet the needs of all, which does not lose too much money, which has high throughput, and is a showpiece

Table 4   Seven categories of people with varying needs and education who may use a joint or dual use facility   Source: Torkildsen 1987

The above points outline some of the major advantages that can be gained from operating a joint provision and dual use scheme. The extent of their success will always depend upon the effectiveness of management policies and procedures and the support of all appropriate staff. However, regardless of how effective management may be, certain difficulties are inherent with the development and operation of these schemes.

◆ DISADVANTAGES OF JOINT ◆
PROVISION AND DUAL USE FACILITIES

◆ Design — schemes have to be considered very carefully with long-term planning and needs of potential users in mind. Joint decisions must be made on flexibility of use so that a more varied programme of activities and events may take place in terms of multi-use. For example, if a spring floor for a gymnasium or sports hall is decided upon, it will restrict its use chiefly to sporting competitions. If additional events need to take place, such as exhibitions and conferences then a more resistant and hard-wearing floor might prove to be more appropriate.

In cases of dual use facilities, these require adaptations on behalf of management, in order to offer as wide a range of activities as possible. Generally, the design of buildings for dual use purposes are orientated for educational requirements and do not cater fully for community use. For example, locker systems vary for adult and children use and the height of showers is also another area of concern for the design of facilities.

◆ Location — The siting or location of joint provision and dual facilities will invariably cause problems. The 'ideal' location may not be possible or planning permission may be rejected. Schools in the main are located on the outskirts of populated areas and therefore, are not accessible to everyone. These problems could be reduced if good public transport facilities existed making accessibility easier and increasing the probability of people using the facilities on offer. This applies more particularly to dual use schemes which are predominantly operated on school premises.

◆ Administration — The administration of any leisure facility is not easy, but it becomes increasingly more difficult when joint provision and dual use schemes are in operation. This mainly stems from the involvement of more than one body or party who have a common interest in the scheme but may adopt different administrative procedures in their management policies. Unless compromises and agreements are reached early, preferably before a scheme is implemented, administrative difficulties will arise.

◆ Finance — Although joint provision and dual use schemes can prove to be economical, financial implications may arise if responsibility for capital and operating costs are not shared with common consensus of all parties involved. Shared responsibilities must also be met in the cost of maintenance, servicing and replacement of equipment so that the scheme can remain functional with minimal or no apparent disruption made to its users. Financial matters can become complex, especially if problems or difficulties arise in making payments.

◆ Staffing — The number of staff required to operate a joint provision or dual use scheme must be considered extremely carefully. Whatever scheme is employed, sufficient staff are required throughout the opening times. This will require a shift-work system, typical for employees in the leisure industry, to be administered, and forward planning will be a managerial necessity.

Having given considerable thought to staff in terms of numbers, there must be sufficient available to provide a quality service in a competitive market. It must be remembered that staff salaries represent the greatest expenditure of any employer. Apart from paying salaries, an employer has to make their employer contribution to cover National Insurance, sickness and holiday entitlements. Additional expenses to the employer may also include pension contributions, overtime and provision of relief staff.

◆ Time allocation to users — A problem that often arises with joint provision and dual use schemes is in allocating time and space to the various users of the facilities. These may include school, youth clubs, coaching sessions, sports clubs, further education establishments, spectator events and any other special requirements.

Setting priorities to these various users can pose problems, for each will make their demands and will plead that their needs are important. Although some agreed policy can be formulated, it would produce inflexibility to change. However, if the scheme is essentially for school use, then the school should be given top priority so that children will obtain the educational benefits they deserve.

◆ Staff attitudes — Since joint provision and dual use schemes will bring together staff from the various parties involved, attitudes will obviously vary. School staff may hold the view that children should be taught in an environment away from adult pressures while others believe that integration is of value. Whatever the various attitudes might be, serious attempts must be made by all parties concerned to become committed to the particular scheme that confronts them, so that they can derive the numerous benefits that are available.

◆ Security — Various security systems and methods require careful planning and design from the very outset. Security should have constant high priority with all staff being very vigilant at all times. Poor security will lead to other problems such as vandalism and graffiti. These acts are prevalent in today's society and remain a constant problem. They can be minimized by good design in the early planning stages, good security, regular supervision and sound management. Whenever these incidents occur, it is advisable to remedy or clean away the results as soon as possible to deter the spread and possible recurrence of such acts.

- Equipment — The supply and maintenance of equipment within joint provision or dual use schemes requires a common agreement between all parties concerned. Funds for the supply, repair and general maintenance of equipment will come from a variety of sources, but the amount each should provide, is generally an ongoing problem. Joint provision and dual use schemes involve excessive use, hence wear and tear of equipment and playing areas, most noticeably football pitches, become common occurrences.

- Access to and within a leisure complex — Car parking and delivery bays are often a problem of joint provision and dual use schemes. Space for emergency services is sometimes blocked through people's ignorance or inadvertent behaviour. These problems become graver when the school and the leisure facilities have special events at the same time, for example, parents evening and a basketball final.

    Some schemes have aggravated problems of access within their leisure centre due to poor design and lack of notices or signs. For example, gaining access to the changing rooms via the licenced bar may not prove a suitable situation.

- Communication — Communications between the various parties involved in a joint provision or dual use scheme is a major problem, since meetings are rarely conducted, especially on the day-to-day operations of the scheme. The Head of PE generally leaves the premises before the centre manager arrives. Both find time a valuable asset and are reluctant to give up their own time voluntarily to discuss the various management implications that their leisure complex might have. Due to the different hours of work between school and recreation centre, staff are rarely available to meet at any one time. Therefore, communication channels break down and this is one area that must be looked into seriously so that better evaluations and greater efficiency can ensue.

- Licensed premises — These obviously present problems for joint provision and dual use schemes due to the presence of schoolchildren. Many people argue that it is unreasonable and irresponsible to have licensed bars on such premises. The inclusion of licensed facilities in leisure complexes and within such schemes requires careful consideration and stricter controls.

◆ MANAGEMENT GUIDELINES FOR ◆ JOINT PROVISION AND DUAL USE SCHEMES

There are many managerial and administrative factors involved in the sound management of joint provision and dual use schemes. It is not possible to give specific details about the management of such schemes because each is unique in character and make up. It is only possible to offer guidelines which have to be adapted to suit a specific scheme.

It is crucial from the very outset that negotiations on all aspects are discussed fully by all parties concerned. Perhaps the most important factor to clarify is the apportioning of capital and running costs between the various parties concerned. This will involve establishing a joint management committee which must make every attempt to work collectively to obtain the maximum mutual benefit that these schemes can offer.

Problems can emerge in deciding who should form the joint management committee. It is vitally important the committee possess the 'right' people who are determined, committed and dedicated to seeing that their particular scheme becomes efficient and successful.

The joint management committee will have a series of responsibilities to fulfil. These include:

- Ensuring terms are mutually accepted by all parties in terms of initial capital outlay and other revenue costs.
- Considering carefully the design and layout of facilities before proceeding with building, and if necessary, seeking expert advice.
- Deciding clearly for whom the provision of facilities are intended and developing a flexible schedule for users.
- Determining from market research the range of facilities and activities which best meet the needs of potential users.
- Ensuring provisions and access are available for handicapped people.
- Establishing a management structure on how the facilities should be operated and administered so maximum use is obtained of all resources for the benefit of all users.
- Ascertaining a philosophy of use in the day-to-day functions and operating procedures of the facilities.
- Setting staffing levels so that policies, aims and objectives of the scheme are fulfilled.
- Determining the scale of charges and other sources of income so users get value for money.
- Establishing a marketing strategy so that optimum use is made of all resources and services.

The above responsibilities highlight the need for relative autonomy within a committee. Failure to function on these lines, may well aggravate some of the many disadvantages outlined in the preceding section. These schemes can resolve their weaknesses and optimize their strengths if the joint management committee is free from friction and the petty jealousies that are sometime present among some members.

◆ Conclusion ◆

There would seem to be no reason why any type of education establishment should not derive benefits from joint provision or dual use schemes. The benefits to all concerned, including local authorities, far outweigh the disadvantages, in that lower capital expenditure, shared running costs and a greater range of quality facilities are possible, which might otherwise not exist. This is particularly prevalent with ever increasing costs in the provision of leisure facilities.

The key to the success of these schemes stems from the human factor. A good working relationship must exist between all staff and officers of all parties involved. Close monitoring and evaluation procedures must be an ongoing process, and their findings must be dealt with promptly so that efficiency is maintained. Torkildsen, 1987, claims that, 'While joint planning and community partnerships make economic and social common sense, they are only advantageous if they work'.

The impact these schemes have had in recent years will continue to develop, and perhaps at a faster rate. If this is the case, it will require leisure personnel to continue and further their managerial skills, so that the disadvantages prevalent in such schemes, are held to a minimum whilst obtaining maximum benefit.

◆ Discussion Questions ◆

1. Distinguish between joint provision and dual use schemes.
2. What advantages are there for all parties involved in operating joint provision facilities?
3. Describe some of the possible problems that may arise during the developing stages of implementing a joint provision scheme.

4. Outline the various category of users that might use a dual use facility. Do you think users would be more restricted if a dual use facility was not in operation?

5. Describe some of the management implications when joint provision or dual use schemes are in operation.

◆ Case study ◆

The recently developed Drayton Community Centre serves the local primary school, college of further education and community. Due to popular demand by several sports clubs, youth and voluntary organizations, requests for the Centre's facilities were becoming more numerous each week.

Mr. L. Lewis, the school's Head of Physical Education, found himself having problems booking for next term's usage of the facilities. This occurred because other groups made their advanced bookings earlier. Mr. Lewis made a formal complaint to his Headmistress, who in turn informed the pupil's parents. Many of the parents expressed their anger and anxiety about the poor level of management exercised.

1. What are the essential issues that this case presents?

2. What solutions are open to Mr. Lewis and how might these be met?

3. How could this incident have been prevented? Indicate your recommendations for the future administration of the centre.

◆ Useful addresses ◆

1. *Arts Council of Great Britain*, 105 Piccadilly, London W1V OAU, tel 071–629 9495.
2. *BBC*, 35 Marylebone High Street, London W1M 4AA, tel 071–580 5577.
3. *British Institute of Management*, Management House, Cottingham Road, Corby, Northants, tel 0536 20422.
4. *British Market Research Bureau Ltd.* (Target Group Index), Saunders House, 53 The Mall, Ealing, London W5 3TE, tel 081–567 3060.
5. *British Tourist Authority/English Tourist Board*, Library, Thames Tower, Blacks Road, Hammersmith, London W6 9EL, tel 081–846 9000.
6. *British Waterways Board*, Melbury House, Melbury Terrace, London NW1, tel 071–262 6711.
7. *Central Council of Physical Recreation*, Francis House, Francis Street, London SW1P 1DE, tel 071–828 3163/4.
8. *Chief Leisure Officers Association*, E.L. Harris, 20 Essex Road, Stevenage, Herts, SG1 3EX, tel 0438 356177.
9. *Civil Aviation Authority*, 45 Kingsway, London WC2, 071–379 7311.
10. *Countryside Commission*, John Dower House, Crescent Place, Cheltenham, Gloucestershire Gl50 3RA, tel 0242 521381.
11. *Countryside Commission for Scotland*, Battleby, Redgorton, Perth, PH1 3EW, tel 0738 27921.
12. *Countryside Commission for Wales*, 8 Broad Street, Newtown, Powys, Wales, tel 0686 26799.
13. *Forestry Commission*, 231 Corstorphine Road, Edinburgh EH12 7AT, tel 031–334 0303
14. *HMSO*, Publications Centre, mail orders, PO Box 276, London SW8 5DT, telephone orders, tel 071–622 3316.
15. *Institute of Baths and Recreation Management*, Gifford House, 36/38 Sherrard Street, Melton Mowbray, Leics LE13 1XJ, tel 0664 65531.
16. *Institute of Groundsmanship*, 19–23 Church Street, The Agora, Wolverton, Milton Keynes, Bucks MK12 5LG, tel 0908 312511.
17. *Institute of Leisure and Amenity Management*, Lower Basildon, Berkshire RG8 9NE, tel 0491 874222.
18. *Leisure Management Magazine*, First Floor Suite, 40 Bancroft, Hitchin, Herts SG5 1LA, tel 0462 33909.
19. *Leisure Studies Association*, Publications, c/o Continuing Education Unit, The Polytechnic of Central London, 35 Marylebone Road, London.
20. *NALGO*, 1 Mabledon Place, London WC1H 9AJ, tel 071–388 2366.
21. *National Coaching Foundation*, 4 College Close, Beckett Park, Leeds LS6 3QH, tel 0532 744802.
22. *Scottish Tourist Board*, Caledonia House, South Gyle, Edinburgh, EH12 9DQ, tel 031–317 7200.
23. *Scottish Sports Council*, Caledonia House, South Gyle, Edinburgh EH12 9DQ, tel 031–317 7200.

24. *Sports Council*, 16 Upper Woburn Place, London WC1H OQP, tel 071–388 1277.
25. *Sports Council of Northern Ireland*, 2A Upper Malone Road, Belfast BT9 5LA, tel 0232 381222.
26. *Sports Council for Wales*, National Sports Centre, Sophia Gardens, Cardiff CF1 9SW, tel 0222 397571.
27. *Sport and Recreation Information Group*, c/o Sports Documentation Centre, Main Library, University of Birmingham, Birmingham B15 2TT, tel 021–414 5843.
28. *Taylor Nelson Monitor*, Taylor Nelson Group, 457 Kingston Road, Ewell, Epsom, Surrey, tel 081–394 0191.
29. *Welsh Tourist Board*, 3 Castle Street, Cardiff, tel 0222 499909.

◆ GENERAL REFERENCES ◆

1. PARKER, S. (1971) *The Future of Work and Leisure*, London: MacGibbon and Kee Ltd.
2. Editorial Advisory Board (1972) *Charter for Leisure*, Leisure Today p. 15.
3. CUTTEN, G. (1929) *The Threat of leisure*, New Haven: Yale University Press.
4. STALEY, E. (March 1976) Leisure and the Struggle for Significance, *Leisure Today, Journal of Physical Education and Recreation*.
5. ERIKSON, E. (1950) Childhood and Society, New York: Norton.
6. STALEY, E. (1975) *Human Needs – Mandate for Professional Preparation*, Proceedings of 1975 Dallas–SPRE Institute, National Recreation and Park Association.
7. DRUKER, P. (1967) *The Effective Executive*, Pan 1970 (UK paperback), London: Harper and Row.
8. HUBER, G.P. (1980) *Managerial decision-making*. Glenview, **111**: 205–212, Scott, Foresman.
9. REDDIN, W. (1970) *Management Effectiveness*. New York: McGraw-Hill.
10. LEWIN, K., LIPPITT, R. and WHITE, R. (1939) Patterns of Aggressive Behaviour in Experimentally Created Social Climates. *Journal of Social Psychology*, **10**: 271.
11. FIEDLER, F. (1967) *A Theory of Leadership Effectiveness*. New York: McGraw-Hill.
12. BLAKE, R. and MOUTON, J. (1978) *The New Management Grid*. Houston: Gulf Publishing.
13. SORRELS, P. and MYERS, B. (May 1983) Comparisons of Group and Family Dynamics, *Human Relations*. 477–490.
14. SHAW, M. (1981) *Group Dynamics: The Psychology of Small Group Behaviour*, 3rd ed., New York: McGraw-Hill.

15. HUCKFELDT, R. (November 1983) Social Contexts, Social Networks, and Urban Neighbourhoods: Environment Constraints of Friendship Choice, *American Journal of Sociology.* 65–78.
16. STEELE, F. (Spring 1983) The Ecology of Executive Teams: A New View of the Top, *Organizational Dynamics.* 65–78.
17. SHERIF, M. and SHERIF, C. (1953) Groups in Harmony and Tension. New York: Harper and Row.
18. SCHACTER, S. (1959) *The Psychology of Affiliation.* Stanford, California: Stanford University Press.
19. BROWN, R. and WILLIAMS, J. (July 1984) Group Identification: The Same Thing to All People? *Human Relations.* 547–560.
20. LEBOEUF, M. (1979) *Working Smart: How to accomplish more in half the time.* New York: McGraw-Hill.
21. ALEXANDER, R.S. (1960) *Marketing Definitions.* Chicago: American Marketing Association.
22. STANTON, W.G. (1975) *Fundamentals of Marketing.* N.Y: McGraw-Hill.
23. KOTLER, P. (1983) *Principles of Marketing,* 2nd Edition.
24. CROUCH, S. (1984) *Market Research for Managers.* London: Heinemann.
25. GOOD, V.C. and SCATES, D.E. (1954) *Methods of Research.* N.Y: Appleton-Century-Croft Inc.
26. BRECH, E.F.L. (ed) (1963) *The Principles and Practice of Management.* Longmans, Green Co. Ltd.
27. FAYOL, H. (1949) *General and Industrial Management.* London: Sir Isaac Pitman & Sons.
28. TAYLOR, F.W. (1949) *Scientific Management.* New York: Harper & Row.
29. PETER, L.J. (1985) *Why Things Go Wrong or The Peter Principle Revisited.* George Allen & Unwin.
30. MAIER, N. (1958) The Appraisal Interview, New York: John Wiley.
31. ASTRAND, PER–OLAF (1972) 'Do we need Physical conditioning?' *Journal of Physical Education* 129–136, Special Edition.
32. The Sports Council (1988) *Into the 90s – A Strategy for Sport 1988–1993.*
33. SESSONS, H.D. (1989) Programmes and Professional Preparation in the 1990's. Presented at the SPRE Educational Institute. New Orleans: Congress of Parks and Recreation.
34. *Sport and Recreation on School Facilities – Joint Provision and Dual Use in the East Midlands* (March 1980) East Midlands Sports Council.
35. *Extending the Use of Existing Facilities* (1982) N.W. Sports Council.
36. *Dual Use of Educational Facilities Seminar – Problems and Potential.* (1987) Sports Council Northern Region.
37. House of Lords Select Committee (1973) Report on Sport and Leisure 2nd Report, London: HMSO.
38. *Sport in the Community: The Next Ten Years* (1982) The Sports Council.
39. *Provision of Facilities for Sport* (1964) Department of Education and

Science and Ministry of Housing and Local Government Joint Circular 11/64 and 49/64. London: DES.
40. *The Chance to Share* (1970) Department of Education and Science : Circular 2/70. London: DES.
41. *Sport and Recreation* (1975) Department of Environment London: HMSO.
42. *Dual Use of Education Facilities* (1976) West Midlands Sports Council.
43. *Sharing Does Work* (1981) The Sports Council Study 21. Coopers and Lybrand Associates Ltd.
44. *Opening Doors – A Dual Use Initiative* (1984) Sports Council and Department of Environment.
45. *Dual Use Turning Policies into Practice.* (Jan 1987) Eastern Council For Sport and Recreation. Report 15.
46. *Optimum Use of School Sports Facilities* (1988) Phase 1 Monitoring Report, The Sports Council For Wales.
47. TORKILDSEN, G. (1987) *Leisure and Recreation Management*, London, E. and F. N. Spon.

◆ Index ◆

administration, 85, 86, 127
advertising, 53, 54, 55, 56, 57, 58, 59
   selection, 57, 58, 59
   targeting, 55
   (see also media)
aerobics, 108, 109, 115
A.I.D.A. principle, 56, 57
Alexander, R., 42, 135
analysis of data, 71, 72
Arts Council, 123, 133
Astrand, P., 136

Blake, R. and Mouton, J., 29, 135
brainstorming, 15, 16
Brech, E., 85, 135
Brown, R. and Williams, J., 135
budget,
   (see promotional budget)

case studies, 10, 23, 40, 67, 83, 101, 117, 118, 132
coach, 11, 38
communication, 17, 18, 19, 20, 50, 129
   additional considerations, 20, 21, 22
   barriers of, 50
   principles of, 17, 18, 19, 20
   the communication square, 21
community leaders, 5
competitive environment, 66, 67
compulsory competitive tendering, 63
computer applications, 105, 106
consultant, 38, 103
Coopers and Lybrand, 123, 136
centralisation, 90
Crouch, S., 69, 72, 135
cultural values, 79
Cutten, G., 4, 134

decentralisation, 90
decision-making, 11
   characteristics, 11
   effective procedures, 14, 15
   group problem-solving techniques, 15, 16, 17
   people and circumstances, 12
   styler, 13
Delphi technique, 16, 17
DES, 121, 122, 136
discussion questions, 9, 22, 39, 66, 82, 100, 117, 131, 132
distribution, (see physical distribution)
Drucker, P., 14, 134
dual use, 119, 120, 121, 122
   (see also Joint Provision)
   advantages, 124, 125, 126
   development, 121, 122, 123, 124
   disadvantages, 127, 128, 129
   management guidelines, 129, 130, 131
   provision, 120

East Midlands Sports Council, 119, 123
Eastern Council for Sport and Recreation, 124
economic environment, 62
Erikson, E., 6, 134
exercise equipment guidelines, 111, 112, 113, 114, 115

facilities
   aerobics, 108, 109, 115

changing rooms, 105
dual use, 19
health and fitness, 103
multi-purpose, 108
outdoor, 109
showers, 105
squash, 108
swimming, 107, 108
Fayol, H., 87, 88, 89, 90, 91, 135
Fiedler, F., 28, 134
fitness testing, 109, 110
flexitime, 3, 4

Gibreth, F., 92, 93
Good, V., and Scater, D., 73, 74, 135
group behaviour, 79, 95
group dynamics, 31, 32, 38

Hawthorne experiments, 94, 95
health and fitness facility considerations, 103
   changing rooms and lockers, 105
   computer applications, 105, 106
   design, 103, 104
   equipment, 97, 106, 111, 112, 113, 114, 115
   facilities, 97, 103, 104, 105, 107, 108, 109
   general amenities, 105
   reception and control, 104
   shower facilities, 105
   specialization, 103, 104
   specific areas, 104, 105, 106, 107, 108, 109
health and fitness programme planning and provision, 109, 110
health and fitness trends and future markets, 115, 116, 117
House of Lords Report 1973, 119, 120, 122, 136
human resources management, 98, 99
   (see also personnel and staffing)

induction, 61, 99
information technology, 43, 105, 106
inner cities, 8

joint provision, 119, 120
   advantages, 124, 125, 126
   development, 121, 122, 123, 124
   disadvantages, 127, 128, 129
   management guidelines, 129, 130, 131
   planning, 120

Kotler, P., 42, 44, 135

leadership, 5, 8, 9, 25, 26
   functions and responsibilities, 26, 27
   theories, 27, 28, 29, 30, 31
   qualities, 25, 26
Le Boeuf, M., 35, 36, 136
leisure,
   definition, 2
   education, 5, 6, 7, 8
   ethic, 7, 8
   future, 8, 9, 117
   management, 85–100
   problems, 4, 5
   sectors, 44
   teaching, 5, 6, 7
Lewin, K., Lippitt, R. and White, R., 27, 28, 134
licensed premises, 129

Index

Maier, N., 100, 136
management
  elements, 88, 89
  functions, 97
  principles, 89
  process, 86, 87
  qualities, 96, 97
  time, 26, 27, 87
managerial grid, 29, 30, 31
managers,
  quality requirements, 96, 97
marketing
  concentrated, 81
  competition, 41, 43
  describing, 41
  differentiated, 81
  mix, 43, 45, 60, 66
  personnel, 60, 61
  phase, 62
  physical distribution, 63, 64
  physical environment, 61, 62
  place, 49
  politeness, 65
  price, 48, 49
  product, 43, 44, 45, 46, 47, 48
  profits, 60, 63
  programme planning, 60, 62, 63
  progress and evaluation, 65, 66
  promotion, 50, 51, 52, 53, 54, 55
  psychological variables, 64
  segmentation, 76, 77, 78, 79, 80, 81
  skills, 41
  strategy, 60, 81
  subsidiary p's, 60
  targeting, 55, 80, 81
  undifferentiated, 80, 81
market research, 69, 70, 71
  experimental method, 71
  observation method, 71
  survey method, 70, 71
Mayo, E., 94, 95
media, 57, 58, 59, 60
  broadcast, 59
  printed, 57, 58
methods engineering, 94
motion economy, 93, 94

Nautilus, 107, 112
needs
  external, 33, 34
  internal, 32
  physiological, 2
  special, 10, 49
nominal group technique, 16
organizational charts, 98
organizations, 86, 87, 88, 89

Parker, S., 1, 2
personnel, 60, 61
  (see also human resources management)
Peter Principle, 96
phase, 60, 62
physical distribution, 60, 63, 64
physical environment, 50, 60, 61
place, 43, 49
Powersport, 107
price, 43, 48, 49, 114

private sector, 44
problem solving, 15
process, 60
product, 43
  life cycle, 46, 47, 51
  mix, 45, 46
  planning, 44, 45
profits, 60, 63
programme planning, 60, 62, 63
progression and evaluation, 60, 65
promotion, 43, 50, 51, 52, 53, 54, 55
promotional budget, 51, 52
psychological variables, 60, 64, 65
public relations, 50, 53, 54
public sector, 44

quality of life, 2
questionnaires, 72, 73, 74
  advantages, 74, 75
  disadvantages, 75, 76
recruitment, 98, 99
Reddin, W., 26, 134
research,
  qualitative, 69
  quantitative, 69
  (see also market research)

scientific management, 91, 92, 93
segmentation,
  behavioural, 78, 79
  demographical, 76, 77
  geographical, 77
  market, 77, 80
  psychological, 77, 78
selling, 54
Sessions, H., 117, 136
social status, 79
sodium lighting, 109
Sport for All, 124
Sports Council, 119, 120, 122, 123, 124, 134, 136
sports development specialists, 5
staffing, 99, 100, 128
Staley, E., 4, 7, 134
Stanton, W., 42, 135

target markets, 55, 80, 81, 82
Taylor, F., 91, 93, 135
teams and team building, 36, 37, 38
  methods, 36, 37
  systematic approach, 37, 38
  television, 6, 53, 55
  relaxation, 6
  sponsorship, 108
time management, 26, 27, 87
time and motion studies, 93
Torkildsen, G., 126, 131, 136
trade exhibition, 51

unity of command, 89
unity of direction, 89, 90

voluntary sector, 44

Wellness movement, 110
work, 1, 2, 3, 32, 35, 36, 61, 93, 94, 95, 96
working with others, 35, 36
work study, 91, 93